*From*
# RENTER
*to*
# OWNER

# From
# RENTER
## to
# OWNER

*Practical, innovative ways
to buy your first home today*

# SUSAN EDMUNDS

ALLEN&UNWIN
SYDNEY • MELBOURNE • AUCKLAND • LONDON

First published in 2023

Text © Susan Edmunds, 2023

Allen & Unwin
Level 2, 10 College Hill, Freemans Bay
Auckland 1011, New Zealand
Phone: (64 9) 377 3800
Email: auckland@allenandunwin.com
Web: www.allenandunwin.co.nz

83 Alexander Street
Crows Nest NSW 2065, Australia
Phone: (61 2) 8425 0100

A catalogue record for this book is available from the National Library of New Zealand.

ISBN 978 1 99100 618 9

Text design by Saskia Nicol
Set in Newsreader
Printed and bound in Australia by the Opus Group

10 9 8 7 6 5 4 3 2 1

*For my kids and their friends, in the hope that homeownership is an achievable goal for them.*

# CONTENTS

Chapter One

**So you want to buy a house . . . 9**

*Why buying a house might be a good idea for you, and
busting some homeownership myths*

Chapter Two

**It's all about the money 29**

*How much might you need for a deposit, and different
ways to reach your savings goal, including making
KiwiSaver work for you*

Chapter Three

**Keeping it in the family 65**

*Might your family / whānau be able to lend a helping
hand? Ways family can support your house purchase*

Chapter Four

**Getting the bank to say yes 99**

*Getting your finances in order: what the bank needs
to see before it will fund your first house*

Chapter Five

**Could your first home be a new house? 139**

*The pros and cons of building a new house*

Chapter Six
**The search for your first home 161**
*Spoilt for choice: what kind of house do you want
to buy?*

Chapter Seven
**Less traditional buying options 183**
*Thinking outside the square: other ways
to property ownership*

Chapter Eight
**Refining your open-home strategy,
and making an offer 209**
*Making all the open home visits count, and what
to do when you find the house of your dreams*

Chapter Nine
**Life with a mortgage, and other costs 239**
*Understanding your loan commitment and the other
costs of homeownership*

Chapter Ten
**Are you ready to become an investor? 265**
*What you need to know about life as a landlord*

Epilogue
**Ready, set, go! 287**
*TLDR and words from the wise!*

**Acknowledgments 303**

**About the Author 304**

Chapter One

# SO YOU WANT TO BUY A HOUSE . . .

Seeing as this is a book about buying your first home, you might expect me to begin with a line about how New Zealanders have a 'love affair' with property.

Or how a quarter-acre section is part of the 'national psyche'.

Or maybe how every young person dreams of buying a house.

I mean, we hear it so often it must be true, right?

But this isn't most books. And, given that you are navigating the New Zealand property market in the third decade of the twenty-first century, after a pandemic propelled prices up by almost 40 per cent in just one year (albeit followed by a somewhat softer drop), you're not typical of 'most' house-buyers.

The truth is that house prices have increased so much over the past decade, even allowing for a few periods of weakness, that things are a bit different now.

Yes, it's true that interest rates are mostly lower than they were when some of our parents bought houses (many borrowers today would faint on the spot if they saw a 20 per cent interest rate from the bank, and even more would end up defaulting on their mortgages).

But on a price-to-income basis – that's how many years of median income it would take to buy a median-priced house – things are significantly harder now for modern buyers than they were for previous generations. You can quote me on that next time an older member of your family tries to tell you otherwise.

In 1975 the average weekly wage was $95 (equivalent to $1119.85 in 2022), or roughly $5000 a year. QV data shows the average house price at the time was $24,300. That means a typical house was about five times an average single income.

In June 2022, the median income for people who were employed was $1189 a week, or $61,828 a year. The median house price across New Zealand was $850,000 – or about 14 times that single median income.

When I first started thinking about buying a house, someone gave me a book that promised to tell me how to pay off my mortgage in no more than five years. It included advice like looking up the price the seller had paid for the home and offering slightly more to cover their costs of selling.

Even then – which feels like a million years ago but is more like 10 – this seemed unlikely to be a successful strategy.

And the idea of paying off a home loan within five years? That might be possible if you borrowed $100,000 and were a couple each earning a good salary. But when you are borrowing a million dollars to get in the door of many Auckland houses, it's pretty far-fetched to expect a loan not to stick around for decades, unless you happen to have a couple of extremely lucky Lotto tickets in your back pocket.

So, that's all a bit depressing. But it means it's time for a new book and a new approach to buying a house. All clichés aside, buying a house is still a big goal for a lot of people and it is still possible, even if it doesn't always feel like it.

Statistics show that first-home buyers are incredibly resilient, all things considered. Whatever the market throws at them, and however unlikely the asking prices seem to be, first-home buyers stick at it. They reliably make up at least a fifth of all purchasers, and sometimes a quarter, according to property insight firm CoreLogic. That held even during the period when CCCfA's (Credit Contracts and Consumer Finance Act) new lending rules came in December 2021 and people had to start accounting for the food they were buying for their dogs.

We seem to be just as ready to sign up for a $700,000-plus loan with a financial instrument that is literally called a 'death pledge' as we were when it took more like $250,000 to get in the door.

### Until death?

*The word 'mortgage' comes from Old French, and Latin before that, and means 'death contract'. The pledge ends (or dies) when the obligation is fulfilled – in this case, the loan is paid off – or the property is seized from the borrower and sold. The 'mortgage' is not the loan itself, it's the agreement that the lender can hold the house as security to make sure the borrower pays what is owed.*

But homeownership isn't for everyone, and not at every stage of life. You might have been told 'the best time to buy was yesterday' but that is only true if it actually suits your circumstances. (It might also be true if the market is crazy and on your side, but that is extremely hard to predict.)

Here are a few things to think about when you work

through whether homeownership is right for you, and if it is, when that might be. No crystal balls are required but it's good to be as honest with yourself as you can.

## Do you worry about having a secure place to live?

Except in relatively rare, and lucky, circumstances, most adults have to pay for a place to live. If you rent, the money that you pay is effectively paying off someone else's home loan, rather than your own.

When you move out, you have nothing to show for the years of payments you've made. You'll get your bond back if your final inspection goes smoothly, and maybe a reference for your cat if you managed to get a landlord to agree to a pet, but that's it.

But when you own a house, even if prices don't rise for a while, you're still paying off your loan and usually building equity over the years. You could see this as a kind of forced savings that should give you a bit of a nest egg at the end of it, in the form of a freehold house.

When you own your home, you won't have a landlord telling you that you must move out because they want to move back in, or that they're putting the house on the market. That extra sense of security is a big deal for lots of people, particularly families with kids. Moving regularly becomes pretty tiring when it means pulling your kids out of familiar surroundings and settling somewhere new.

And most of the time, in most parts of the country, it's not that hard to sell your house if you do find you need to move or that the security we just talked about isn't actually a good thing for you.

Usually, you can put your house on the market and, provided the price is right and there are no major problems with the property, you can find a buyer. You won't always make a lot of money but you should be able to move on. In that way, homeownership can be quite flexible and not the permanent tie you might have thought it was.

You can also rent your property out if you buy it and then find you have to move somewhere else for a while, which gives you an investment and a way back into the local area if you return. (There are some rules around doing this if you have used KiwiSaver to purchase your property, which I'll cover in the next chapter.)

## *Equity*

*Equity is your stake in the house. To work out your equity, take the current value of the property and deduct the amount you owe on it. If you bought the house yesterday with a 10 per cent deposit, you have 10 per cent equity. As the house's value rises, and you pay down your loan, your equity in the house increases.*

## Do you want to limit the amount you pay for your home in the future?

Rents tend to rise year after year, so the amount you have to pay for your home will increase.

That's not always a huge problem if you are earning and if you are getting solid pay rises as you progress through your career, but it can be a major issue when you retire and are on more of a fixed budget. If you pay off your house by the time you retire, it puts you in a much better position for a comfortable, less stressful retirement.

While rent can keep rising, the amount you owe on your house will not increase unless you borrow more. True, interest rates do move around a lot but, as we've seen in recent years, they go down as well as up, so you will get a reprieve from time to time.

Over time, inflation makes the amount you paid for your house, and any remaining mortgage on it, seem small.

You only need to look at old house ads from the 1970s or 1980s to see how much prices change (and probably curse yourself for not being alive or not earning enough pocket money at the time to buy a home in one of the leafier suburbs).

In the 1970s, roughly $20,000 was a pretty typical house price. A news article on *Stuff* in 2021 followed a house that in 1975 was for sale for offers over $36,000. It sold again for $1.1 million in July 2019.

## Do you want to paint your living room walls chartreuse?

When you own your own home, you can pretty much do exactly what you want with it, as long as it fits within the council rules and any restrictions that come with your subdivision. (I currently live in a subdivision that doesn't allow boundary fences, which is its own kind of nightmare when you have a small and energetic dog.)

But if you want to paint your living room walls orange, green or every colour of the rainbow, no one will question it, unless you have seriously judgemental friends.

You'll also be able to do things like plant fruit trees knowing that you can choose to stick around to see them fruit, and you can have pets without drafting up a resume and cute little passport photo for them to get them past any future landlords.

While homeownership rates have dropped since the 1990s, they have held pretty steady since the 2010s, even though house prices soared. That indicates that for lots of people, the tangible and intangible benefits of homeownership are still tantalising enough for it to make sense.

Economist Gareth Kiernan says homeownership is still a good goal to strive for.

'There are lots of positives tied up with home-ownership: security of tenure; 'forced savings' through paying the mortgage; the acquisition of a valuable asset over time; and reduced accomm-odation costs in retirement.

'Owning your own property is generally a good hedge against inflation and if the value of the property rises, the tax-free capital gains are going to outperform most other investment options, especially when you have a mortgage, so you're banking the returns leveraged from someone else's money.'

That might sound a bit like finance-speak, so let me break it down into normal English.

Say you buy an $800,000 house with a 10 per cent deposit, which is $80,000.

If the house increases in value by 10 per cent over a year, you basically double your money because even though you only put in 10 per cent of the purchase price, all the gains are yours. It'd be hard to find a better investment – if you had invested that $80,000 in the share market and made a 10 per cent return, you'd only have an additional $8000.

When the housing market is hot, you've probably seen news stories about the average house making more in a year than the average worker.

For several years, until the start of 2022, we had a long run of really strong price increases, which made people who own houses feel better off, at least on paper. While those increases did stop, the trend over the years is still clearly up.

Of course, it's all a bit academic because you can't actually spend those gains unless you sell your house and you either have somewhere to live free of charge, or you're moving somewhere much cheaper. But an increase in your house's value boosts your equity position overall, which can help if you want to join the infamous ranks of property investors, and helps you keep pace with the market.

Kiernan notes that with house prices as high as they are, it's harder than ever to save a deposit, especially in relation to incomes.

He says anyone who was trying to save in 2020 and 2021 probably saw themselves getting further from their target rather than closer to it. But things started to improve through 2022 and Kiernan points out that there are ways to get in the door, even if you don't have the money upfront: co-ownership schemes, help from family, buying a brand-new property requiring a smaller deposit, or moving to cheaper parts of the country, like Canterbury. No shade, Canterbury – in 2021, Christchurch had the best income-to-house price ratio of any of the cities in the country.

I'll cover how these, and other options, can work for you a bit later on.

But there's some other stuff to think about, too.

You are committing yourself to a huge investment when you buy a house. For some people, that's a bit of a concern, especially when house prices shot up at an enormous rate over the past decade, and despite some softening are still elevated beyond what many people think is sustainable. Sometimes even the amount of interest that you'll pay over the 20 or 30 years of a mortgage can make you feel nauseous.

While I don't think huge numbers of people will be trapped long-term in houses in which they are underwater on their loans and cannot afford to sell, it's a good idea to consider how the commitment of homeownership sits with you.

If you like to move around (I once moved flats nine times in two years, for little reason other than people kept offering me slightly cheaper rent), or you have a job that requires you to be able to pick up and move for the sake of your career, you might decide that buying a house is not a good option for you, at least not right now.

While property has generally been a good investment, it's not a sure bet. You could find house prices were soft at the time you wanted to sell, or that buyer demand was down. It's buyer demand that tends to drive prices. If there are no buyers in the market, sellers who really need to sell have to reduce their prices to find them. We saw this through 2022 when sales slowed a lot. People who bought at the end of 2021 would have had difficulty selling with any money left over.

The more serious you are about selling, the more you might have to drop your price to meet the soft market.

The key to not losing money is not to get to the point where you are desperate to sell. Usually that happens to people who have lost work or had their income fall away.

But you can lose money on a house for a lot of reasons – maybe the house has an undiscovered fault that you can't fix, a major roading project changes your neighbourhood or your neighbours decide they are going to teach five-year-olds to play the violin all day from a new structure in their back garden that completely blocks your sunshine.

There are also legal costs associated with buying and selling, and real estate commission. If you buy and sell regularly, or sell not long after you bought, these costs can erode any gains in price you might make.

While you can often give notice and move out of a rental property within a matter of weeks, when it comes to selling you usually have at least a month of preparations and open homes, and that's if everything goes smoothly. Then you'll have to wait at least another month before settlement and the property changes hands.

Once you own a house, you're also on the hook for all the maintenance requirements, and council rates. There's no landlord to ring if you find water leaking through the light fittings. This is fine if you're relatively confident when it comes to DIY, but if no one living in your house has any practical skills, you will also need to budget for calling the experts.

Shamubeel Eaqub, another economist who's often in my phone's recent contacts, has long warned against New Zealanders' obsession with buying houses. He told me in 2012 that it wasn't a good time to buy, but we won't hold that against him.

He thinks house prices became overstretched in 2022 in most parts of the country, compared to previously when it was mainly the centres of Auckland, Wellington, Queenstown and Nelson which were high. 'We now have population growth in previously zombie towns and they are not coping with the sudden reversal in population fortunes.'

But after all that (is your head spinning yet?), watch out for your brain trying to fool you into thinking you shouldn't buy. Our brains are pretty good at trying to protect us and identifying threats even before we're conscious of them. Sometimes they try to identify threats that aren't really there at all – particularly when they're approaching with large debts attached.

There are a few myths that might trick you into thinking you can't, or even don't want to, buy a house – when that's not actually the case.

If you are on the verge of checking out and deciding buying a house is just too hard, make sure you're not falling for any of these myths:

## Myth one: It's impossible for anyone right now

There's a lot of talk in the media about how hard it is to buy a house. But I've been working as a business and personal-finance journalist for more than a decade and I remember stories of that nature the entire time. Sometimes its that the deposit hurdle is very high, sometimes it's that interest rates have shot up.

Taking these messages to heart could make you think you might as well just give up and buy a tent to set up on your parents' back lawn. But don't despair. Even when banks clamped down on lending and we had people saying they were being turned away even when they had a 60 per cent deposit (yes, really), still a fifth of all sales were to someone who had not owned a house before. People do it. You can do it.

Note: that does not mean 'anyone' can do it. You do need to have a solid income and good savings history. See the next chapter for more on that.

## Myth two: House prices are going to drop dramatically any minute, so I'll wait

When house prices are high, talk turns to the fact that there's a 'bubble' and house prices are due to crash.

That's scary to hear, particularly if you're pondering the prospect of a huge home loan. The problem is that people have been saying this for years. The drop we experienced through 2022 is one of the biggest in decades, in nominal terms (that is, when you don't take inflation into account). But it still didn't take prices back to where they were in 2019.

If you had bought a house just before prices dropped coming out of the Global Financial Crisis of 2007–8, you would still probably be pretty happy today even though prices took five years to recover to their previous peak. There are still people waiting for the huge drop that never came. Hanging on and waiting for a price drop isn't a safe bet unless you have a reliable crystal ball.

## Myth three: It's hard now so owning a home will be a hard slog forever

When you first buy, it's likely that your mortgage payments will seem like a bit of a stretch. They are probably more than your rent payments. But over time, your income should rise, which should make the payments more affordable.

You might get a promotion. Your business might take off. Things should improve. Loss aversion is often talked about in finance – it describes our tendency to feel losses more keenly than gains. People who worry about losing out now can end up costing themselves a lot in the long run. Be careful not to let loss aversion worries about paying a mortgage make you miss out on what could work out to be a good investment.

# BUYER STORY:
## Shai

Shai, an Auckland lawyer in her thirties, spent almost a year trying to buy her first house before settling on one in Riverhead.

She was able to buy because of an inheritance, and because she had saved in KiwiSaver for more than a decade.

It was a daunting process. Prices increased by double-digit percentages during the period she was looking for a home.

She says there were two main reasons that homeownership still appealed to her, despite the seemingly insurmountable challenge: the financial consideration of being 'in' the market that is a big driver of the country's wealth, and the stability it would give her family.

'Owner-occupiers are growing their wealth all the time because the value of their property is increasing at alarming speeds every year,' Shai says. 'At the same time, the cost of renting has been rising faster than incomes for the last 30 years. For many people, their incomes have stagnated and living costs are rising steeply.'

She says that people talk almost disparagingly about 'FOMO' – young people wanting to get into property because they have a fear of missing out. But Shai can relate and says it's actually a really sensible worry.

'People can see, rightly or wrongly, that simply owning a house grows your wealth more than most people can hope to earn by working really hard. Renters often face a future where their ability to save money continues to shrink and it takes longer and longer to get themselves into a better situation.

'For me, the biggest driver is stability. The immature tenancy laws we have in this country mean you are totally at the whim of your landlord as to how long you may or may not be able to stay anywhere.

'There is that constant uncertainty about your end date in any given house, no matter how great your landlord is – and we've been fortunate in the last year-and-a-half to have a good one. Regardless, there's the uncertainty that they could choose to move back into the house at any point, or sell it, or want a family member to move in. There are so many reasons why good landlords, let alone the awful property managers out there, decide to end tenancies.

'For me, I wanted to make sure my children can have a stable life like I was fortunate enough to have. I didn't have to move many times like young children have to these days.'

Shai says she doesn't think of herself as a struggling first-home buyer because she was in a stable rental situation while looking for a home. She and her husband have two high incomes coming into the household, and they have been saving for a long time.

'We are certainly far better off than many but we still didn't find it easy. It's hard going to auctions knowing very well that at the end of the day you can't really compete with the amount of equity that anyone in Auckland has if they happened to own their house for a couple of years. We were on the ground looking at houses and constantly getting pushed out of suburbs.'

The search for an affordable home pushed them further and further from the central city, she says. It felt like with each month that ticked by they had to move their search to a suburb a little further away.

'The speed at which we were getting priced out of places was amazing. Sometimes I wish we had taken a real dud earlier.'

She says they decided against that option because they worried there would be too little cash left after the mortgage to put into a do-up.

'We wouldn't have had the money left over to do that. I don't think the older generations understand that point, as they're always saying,

"Oh we used to buy houses and fix them up."'

Shai says the other thing she wishes she had was a time machine.

'I wish I'd decided five years ago that I was going to buy a house. The only option I would tell young renters now is if they can ever get themselves in a situation where there's four or five of them, if they can start to think that you don't need to be in a couple to buy a house, maybe just buy a house with friends if you're going to flat with them anyway. I know a group of people who did that earlier this year and it's actually more attainable than you think.'

She says people often think if they're in a flatting situation, living with a lot of people, homeownership is out of reach, but it's not as much of a stretch as some might think. Shai says if she'd done that, she could be in a better situation now. 'There are not enough conversations around what alternative ownership models might look like. In 2015 we thought that house prices were mad and it couldn't get worse, but now people would love to be dealing with prices from 2015.'

# Chapter Two

# IT'S ALL ABOUT THE MONEY

The main thing that's standing between you and the home of your dreams is probably money. Maybe a lot of it.

To get in the door, almost all first-home buyers need someone to lend them the money to make the deal happen. And in the vast majority of cases, that someone is a bank, and the lending is a mortgage.

This can be daunting if the extent of your interactions with your bank to date has been to take out a credit card and maybe organise an overdraft if you struggled from payday to payday in your first job.

But, luckily for you, home loans are a big part of every bank's business model and, while you might be looking at a sum of money that seems unimaginably enormous to you right now, home loans are the sort of things that lenders deal with every day.

To get a home loan approved, there are two major things you need to tick off. The first is to show you have enough of a deposit saved to be eligible for a loan. The second is to demonstrate that you can service the mortgage – that is, make all the repayments for however many decades it takes you to pay it off – once you have bought the house.

First up, let's have a look at how you can pull that deposit together.

## Saving a deposit (otherwise known as the biggest financial goal you've probably ever tackled)

In recent years, saving the deposit part of the home loan equation has been particularly difficult for lots of first-time buyers.

Because house prices have been rising pretty quickly, and interest rates have been relatively low, the amount required for a deposit has also been rising at a faster rate than many people have been able to save.

When house price increases are happening faster than wage growth, it means people who are saving a deposit have to work extra hard.

But people do make it work. House price momentum

faltered after the Covid craziness, allowing wages to catch up at least a little – albeit from quite a way behind – and there are always ways to save money, even if it all seems a little daunting at the outset.

Lots of studies show that people overestimate what they can achieve in the short term but underestimate what they can do over a longer period. If you set an ambitious yet realistic savings goal, you might not be able to achieve it immediately, but it might still be within your reach in the longer term.

There are a few common ways that people save deposits.

## KiwiSaver

If you are a potential first-home buyer, KiwiSaver is probably your friend. If you're not already a member, you should get in now. Yes, it's a way to save, but it also unlocks a number of benefits that could help you buy your first home.

One of the most common ways of saving a deposit for a first home, or supplementing the savings you have, is through KiwiSaver. While the scheme was set up to help us provide for ourselves in retirement, it clearly now has a dual aim because it helps thousands of first-home buyers every month.

If you are an employee of a New Zealand company, and you want to buy a house to live in in this country, making the most of KiwiSaver is really a no-brainer.

You probably have a pretty good understanding of how the scheme works. It's been the hot topic of personal finance articles since it launched in 2007.

Very briefly: if you are an employee, you pay a minimum of 3 per cent of your salary into your KiwiSaver account. Your employer also makes a minimum 3 per cent contribution. (Some employers are a bit stingy and count their contribution as part of your 'total remuneration package', which means you are effectively contributing 6 per cent but are supposedly paid more to compensate for this. If you don't think this arrangement is working well for you, you could take it up with your employer.)

Most people make the minimum contribution of 3 per cent, matched by an employer's 3 per cent, but there are options to increase your own contribution and some employers are more generous.

Over time, this can be a great way to save money. You and your employer both pitch in and because KiwiSaver is an investment, rather than a savings account, you can tweak how your money is invested to maximise your returns.

If you plan to save for five years or more, you might opt for a growth fund, which will give you more exposure to equities (the sharemarket). Returns from these funds can be a bit bumpy but should deliver for you over time. If you plan to buy sooner than five years, you might choose a less risky fund – but it should still give you a higher return than you would get by keeping your money in the bank.

When it comes time to withdraw from your KiwiSaver account, you can take out all the money in your fund except for $1000. You might also qualify for some free money from the government. More on that in a minute.

KiwiSaver has the benefit of being out of sight. If you get your investment settings right at the outset – you can ask a financial adviser for help with this or hit up your KiwiSaver provider – you can leave it to tick over in the background, slowly growing and getting ready for you to call on it when the time comes.

You don't have to worry about what investments your KiwiSaver is making (that's the fund manager's job) and there is no chance of you tapping into it and undoing your hard work of saving, because the money is locked up until it is time to buy your house, or retire, whichever happens first. Let's hope it's the house.

To withdraw your KiwiSaver money, you'll need to intend to live in the property for at least six months.

## How much should you contribute to KiwiSaver?

If you haven't tweaked your KiwiSaver settings, it's likely that your KiwiSaver is set at a default 3 per cent contribution. This isn't bad, but it won't put you on the fast track to saving a house deposit.

If you earn $70,000 a year and save 3 per cent of that, plus another 3 per cent from your employer, and you are in a balanced fund, you will save about $23,000 in three years. If you increase your contribution to 10 per cent of your income, you could save more than $50,000 in the same period of time.

Mortgage broker Glen McLeod tells me he sees people pulling together some serious chunks of money in their KiwiSaver accounts.

'Some people have been saving for a long time, but others, for example a couple who just put their head down and bum up and stop spending and save hard, and if they've put their KiwiSaver payments up from 3 per cent to 8 per cent and they've done that for 12 months, it really rockets the funds up. It's a seriously good addition to a deposit.'

## What sort of KiwiSaver fund gets a house deposit the fastest?

When it comes to saving a house deposit in KiwiSaver, not all funds are created equal.

If you haven't actively chosen the KiwiSaver fund you want to be in, you'll probably find you're in a balanced fund. People used to be defaulted into conservative funds, but recent rule changes now mean that a balanced fund is the default option for people who didn't make a decision. These funds have a mix of high-growth and 'safe' assets.

The problem with 'safe' assets like cash deposits and low-yielding bonds is that, while they are not risky in the way that shares can bump around and gain or lose value, over time you might actually go backwards, particularly when inflation is running hot. This is because your investment might not keep up with inflation or house price growth.

So, if you have a few years to save, consider taking a bit more risk. Investing in a riskier fund means you may see your balance drop as well as grow, but over time you should end up better off.

Take that example of someone earning $70,000 and contributing 10 per cent. If they shift from a balanced fund to a growth fund, they could end up with an additional $3000 over three years, without putting any extra money in themselves. If markets are on their side, they could end up even better off.

But because growth investments can be a bit volatile, as you get closer to taking your money out it is probably a good idea to move back to a less risky option to be more certain of what your account balance will be when you withdraw your money. Your provider or adviser can help to work out the best settings for you.

Some investment funds are designed specifically for first-home savings. For example, BNZ has one that is made up of primarily income (lower-risk) assets.

# KiwiSaver's hidden perks

You know the obvious benefits of KiwiSaver – your employer makes contributions, you can't accidentally spend your savings, the government chips in with $520 a year ... but there are other ways that you can use KiwiSaver to get in the door.

The two main benefits are the First Home Grant and the First Home Loan. If you qualify, these can be a really big help to get into a first home. Here's how they work.

## First Home Grant

The First Home Grant gives you up to $5000 towards an existing home, or $10,000 for a new build. If you are buying as part of a couple, you can both claim that amount, which potentially gives you up to $20,000 to add to your deposit.

To qualify, you need to have been a contributing member of KiwiSaver for at least three years. You don't have to contribute for three years consecutively, but you do have to have contributed for at least three years over the time you have been a member.

Sometimes, people who are on maternity leave get caught out by this contribution requirement because, while they have been a member for three years or more, their contributions might have stopped during the period they were out of the workforce.

If you are out of work for a while and are worried about missing out, you can make voluntary payments. These do not have to be at the same level as when you were working, but they must be equal to the lower of at least 3 per cent of what an adult on the minimum wage would make in a 40-hour week, or $1000 a year. If you are self-employed or on a benefit, your voluntary contributions need to be the lower of at least 3 per cent of your income or $1000 annually, for three years.

The amount you get depends on how long you have been in the scheme. You qualify for $1000 per year (for existing houses) or $2000 per year (for new houses) for every year you've been in the scheme, up to a maximum number of five years.

There are a few conditions to be eligible for the grant: you need to be over 18, not currently own any other property, be earning less than the income cap, buy a house that is within the price cap for the region you are buying in and you must agree to live in it for at least six months.

The income cap for single people is $95,000 before tax. A couple or a single person with no dependents can earn a combined $150,000. The income cap and the property price cap for your region are reviewed every six months.

You'll also need to provide evidence that you have a deposit of at least 5 per cent, including from your

KiwiSaver, money in the bank or money from family.

If your spouse or partner owns a house that you could reasonably be expected to live in or sell, this can be an issue when applying for the First Home Grant. If you are buying with other people, you need to be purchasing an equal share of the property, and if you purchase privately – that is, directly from the owners without using a real estate agent – you may need to prove that you paid a fair price. In this situation, you may be asked to provide a valuation from a registered valuer.

## First Home Loan

The First Home Loan is arguably an even bigger help to get you in the door of your first home, provided you meet the income cap. The government removed the house price caps in the 2022 Budget.

If you qualify, you can access a mortgage with only a 5 per cent deposit. That means, if you're buying an existing house in Whangārei, for example, for $600,000, you only need $30,000 deposit.

The government says it will assess the income caps every six months, which should help – at the moment mortgage brokers say it could be a stretch for people to service a mortgage big enough to buy in some of the main centres while remaining within the income caps.

Borrowing with a low deposit is possible in the

First Home Loan scheme because the loans are underwritten by the government, which means there is less risk for the lender.

You need to meet the government requirements for the loan, and you will also need to get past the lender's own criteria. These criteria can vary depending on who you go through – lenders who offer the scheme include Westpac, Kiwibank, NZCU and NZ Home Loans. Generally, though, lenders will be looking at your ability to repay the loan, the amount of debt you already have, how you manage your money and your credit history.

While the loan is underwritten by the government, you will also need to pay a lender's mortgage insurance premium of 1 per cent of the total loan amount, although this can usually be added into the amount you are borrowing.

McLeod says that if you have a 10 per cent deposit and are borrowing under the First Home Loan scheme, you can usually access banks' specials, discounted rates and some 'cash back' with the deal to help pay your legal costs. However, if you have a deposit less than 10 per cent, you might not be able to access the best interest rates and you probably won't be in line for any cash.

As with the First Home Grant, you cannot use a First Home Loan to buy an investment property. You will need to live in the home for at least six months, and you need to be a citizen, permanent resident, or resident visa-holder normally resident, in New Zealand.

Kāinga Ora, the government agency responsible for housing, administers both of these schemes, as well as a shared equity option, First Home Partner.

To qualify for First Home Partner, you also need to have 5 per cent saved and household income of no more than $130,000. This could be an option if your current deposit and ability to borrow are not sufficient to get you into the house that is right for you. I'll explain more of how this works in the next chapter.

# First Home Loan and First Home Grant price caps (from Budget 2022)

| Region | Existing properties ($) | New build properties ($) |
|---|---|---|
| Far North District | 400,000 | 675,000 |
| Whangārei District | 600,000 | 800,000 |
| Kaipara District | 525,000 | 875,000 |
| Auckland | 875,000 | 875,000 |
| Thames–Coromandel District | 875,000 | 925,000 |
| Hauraki District | 525,000 | 525,000 |
| Matamata–Piako District | 625,000 | 625,000 |
| Hamilton Urban Area | 650,000 | 725,000 |
| Ōtorohanga District | 400,000 | 500,000 |
| South Waikato District | 400,000 | 500,000 |
| Waitomo District | 400,000 | 500,000 |
| Taupō District | 575,000 | 575,000 |
| Tauranga Urban Area | 800,000 | 875,000 |
| Rotorua District | 525,000 | 525,000 |
| Whakatāne District | 500,000 | 500,000 |
| Kawerau District | 625,000 | 625,000 |
| Ōpōtiki District | 400,000 | 500,000 |
| Gisborne District | 450,000 | 500,000 |
| Wairoa District | 400,000 | 500,000 |
| Napier–Hastings | 625,000 | 825,000 |
| Central Hawke's Bay District | 500,000 | 500,000 |
| New Plymouth District | 525,000 | 675,000 |
| Stratford District | 400,000 | 525,000 |
| South Taranaki District | 400,000 | 500,000 |

| | | |
|---|---|---|
| Ruapehu District | 400,000 | 500,000 |
| Whanganui District | 425,000 | 500,000 |
| Rangitīkei District | 400,000 | 500,000 |
| Manawatū District | 525,000 | 525,000 |
| Palmerston North City | 575,000 | 700,000 |
| Tararua District | 400,000 | 500,000 |
| Horowhenua District | 525,000 | 650,000 |
| Wairarapa | 575,000 | 800,000 |
| Wellington Urban Area | 750,000 | 925,000 |
| Nelson–Tasman | 650,000 | 875,000 |
| Marlborough District | 550,000 | 575,000 |
| Kaikōura District | 700,000 | 700,000 |
| Buller District | 400,000 | 500,000 |
| Grey District | 400,000 | 500,000 |
| Westland District | 400,000 | 500,000 |
| Hurunui District | 425,000 | 500,000 |
| Christchurch Urban Area | 550,000 | 750,000 |
| Ashburton District | 400,000 | 500,000 |
| Timaru District | 400,000 | 500,000 |
| Mackenzie District | 500,000 | 500,000 |
| Waimate District | 400,000 | 500,000 |
| Waitaki District | 400,000 | 500,000 |
| Central Otago District | 525,000 | 800,000 |
| Queenstown Lakes District | 875,000 | 925,000 |
| Dunedin City | 500,000 | 675,000 |
| Clutha District | 400,000 | 500,000 |
| Southland District | 500,000 | 500,000 |
| Gore District | 400,000 | 500,000 |
| Invercargill District | 400,000 | 500,000 |

## Kāinga Whenua loan

The Kāinga Whenua loan scheme is designed to help Māori build houses on multiple-owned land.

Traditionally banks have been reluctant to lend on Māori land because it is hard for them to take the property as security.

A Kāinga Whenua loan is secured only against the house, not the house and land.

Kiwibank approves and provides the loans, and there are some restrictions, such as the house area has to be at least 50 square metres, be built on piles and have reasonable road access.

## Other investment strategies

KiwiSaver is an excellent tool to save a first-home deposit, but it will not be the full solution for lots of people. You might want to investigate other ways to boost your wealth to help you get to your goal.

A popular strategy is to set up an investment account to put some money into shares alongside your other savings. Online platforms such as Sharesies, Hatch and Stake have made this a lot easier in recent times.

You can set up an automatic payment to go out of your transaction account each payday and into your investment account, then design an effective investment strategy that fits with your goals.

You'll need to acknowledge upfront that investing in shares does carry some risk, particularly if you're investing money directly in specific companies rather than spreading it across funds that invest in a number of companies, such as the top 50 companies on the NZ Stock Exchange. It can be easy, especially when returns have been good for a while, to expect that will continue.

As you get nearer to your goal and are thinking about withdrawing the money, it could be a good idea to 'de-risk' your investments, maybe by selling out of shares and shifting your cash to more conservative managed funds. The online investment platforms usually make that relatively easy to do.

You can also choose to put your money into term deposits. During periods when interest rates are low, term deposits become less attractive. Sometimes the amount you receive from a term deposit isn't enough to cover inflation – that's the same risk I mentioned earlier with conservative KiwiSaver funds. But if you can get a reasonable rate, are feeling cautious or know you want to buy within a few months, they could be a good option.

Hannah McQueen founded financial coaching firm enable.me, which helps a lot of first-home buyers. She says she arms people with an investment plan for their deposit savings, usually using managed funds, and suggests it's not a good idea to dabble in the sharemarket by yourself if you're hoping to save a substantial amount of money.

She also gives her clients a plan for how long it should take to reach the goal they are striving for. Because the amounts required for deposits are much bigger than they used to be, and interest rates are quite a lot lower, it's not enough to just put money aside in the bank and hope for the best.

'We can no longer afford to keep the money in the bank, chipping away,' McQueen says. 'We've had to bring in our investment team to design investment strategies for these clients. It feels premature, for their age – normally that's something we would do once you're mortgage-free. It's historically linked to older people at a wealthier point in life, but this is more because we can't afford to leave the money sitting there.'

She is relaxed about people with $10,000 or so managing their own investments, but says once you get to $50,000 or more it's a good idea to get some expert advice.

'It's getting the money working harder, and then working sharper again, working out what's needed.'

She recommends people save no less than 20 per cent of their after-tax income.

Sometimes, the people she deals with can pay

off all their debts and get to that level of saving in a relatively short period of time. Others take a bit longer to get on track.

'They've got to get lean before they get fit. They're often carrying a lot of bad habits, and have a lack of strategy or the wrong behaviour or systems. They're not deliberate about anything so it normally takes about three months of intensively trying to explain to them what's needed and putting them through their paces. Some clients are saving 20 per cent of their income within three months, some can take 12 months to get to that point. We ultimately want to get them saving 30 per cent.'

McQueen says people often want to know that they're able to achieve something in return for the sacrifices they're making.

'Once they can see that it makes a difference, people will make a sacrifice – if they can see the return is guaranteed for the effort. No one wants to make a sacrifice when they don't believe in it.'

## That 'b' word

It's likely that you'll need to spend a couple of months before you put in your application to the bank making sure that your bank accounts look relatively tidy.

This doesn't mean living on two-minute noodles

and never leaving the house except to work.

But it does mean making an effort to show that you live within your means and could cope with the extra home loan repayment when it comes your way. You'll need to formulate a decent household budget and then show that you can stick to it.

McLeod says he tells people who are more profligate spenders, willing to get their credit cards out more often, that they need to cut back. 'If it's just going out and having a life, they need to curb that for a bit.'

He says some people don't find it hard to knuckle down and behave themselves financially for a bit, but other would-be buyers need to set up controls like a bank account that needs two signatures before money can be withdrawn.

He says people shouldn't be afraid to celebrate their successes on the way to a big goal like a first-home deposit.

'When you hit your first $10,000, have a bottle of wine. You need to acknowledge that you are getting there. If you tuck it away and it's a hard grind, you become a bit resentful. You need your mindset in the right place: "I'm going to buy a home". It might take three to five years to save enough for a deposit, so do what you need to do, but make sure you have smaller goals along the way where you can tick the box and congratulate yourself for the hard work you've done.

'And if you can't do it in a way that you feel you

can protect the funds yourself, chuck it in your KiwiSaver.'

## What if you're your own boss?

When you're self-employed, things can be a bit different. You can still contribute to KiwiSaver – and you might choose to do this either through voluntary payments when it suits you, or from a salary if you pay yourself one. You won't get an employer contribution (or if you do put one through, it's from yourself as well so it's a bit less of a bonus) but you will still qualify for the $520 tax credit from the government each year you contribute at least $1042. That means it's worth putting in at least that basic amount, but how you choose to save beyond that amount is up to you. You might like the discipline and hands-off nature of KiwiSaver or you might want to work with an investment adviser to build your wealth elsewhere.

When it comes time to apply for a loan, you can expect to have to answer a few more questions as a self-employed person. You will need to be able to prove that your business earns a solid income, and is likely to continue to do so, to ensure that you can keep up with the repayments you are signing on to make. Usually, this means providing two full years' worth of end-of-year financial statements so a lender can see what is going on in your business's financial life. The financial statements will need to include a profit and loss statement, a cash flow statement and a balance sheet for the business. Your accountant probably prepares these statements for you.

If your business is new and you don't have two years' worth of financial statements to show, you could ask your accountant to draw up a cash flow forecast based on how you are already performing, which the lender can use to gauge the likelihood of future profitability. If you have signed any contracts for upcoming work, you could also include these as part of your application.

If you know you're going to be applying for a mortgage soon, it might be useful to think about what your business's books look like. Sometimes, businesspeople claim significant expenses, which reduces their tax obligations. But it can also make the business look less financially healthy.

Sometimes, self-employed people who are turned away from a bank because they don't yet have a strong track record have more success with a non-bank lender. They can then refinance their loan with a bank when they have their paperwork in order.

## Other options

Every so often, a new product enters the market that is meant to make it easier for first-home buyers to get together a deposit or buy a house. When I was in my early twenties, there were a lot of people advertising a product that was an 80 per cent loan from a main bank and a 20 per cent high-interest 'deposit' loan from a second-tier lender.

This didn't last long as it was a pretty expensive option for people wanting to buy a house at what turned out to be the peak of that market cycle.

One recent product is Squirrel's Launchpad, which does something a little similar. It offers borrowers a base loan of 80 per cent of the house purchase price, initially set up as an interest-only loan for five years, which works like a traditional mortgage. It then adds an equity loan of up to $120,000 or another 15 per cent of the property, whichever is lower, which works like a personal loan, on top. The interest rate is a lot higher than the base loan but the term of the loan is only five years.

In five years' time, you should have paid off the more expensive loan and be left only with the 80 per cent mortgage on the house.

Squirrel has been pretty clear that this product is aimed at people who have good incomes but have struggled to get the money together for a deposit. It won't suit everyone. It's worth thinking about how products like this perform if prices fall.

Sometimes, banks offer products that are designed to help you save to get into a home. It's important to look closely at these products to really understand what they offer, because there can be hidden costs (and benefits). For example, when banks are restricting their lending they often prioritise existing customers over applications from new ones. But quite often you can set up the same structure (without the 'first home' label) from whichever lender you prefer, and avoid fees or other restrictions that may come with the product.

BNZ offers a first-home-buyer KiwiSaver fund but it is invested quite conservatively and intended for people who plan to withdraw their money within the next three years. If you're saving over a longer period, it's worth getting advice on whether this sort of investment is right for you.

# BUYER STORY:
## Shara and Sherman

Shara and her partner, Sherman, bought their first home in Whangārei while they were both still working at the local supermarket.

Shara was 23 and studying to be a nurse when they purchased in 2020.

'When I was in my first year of study we were able to get a rental but the landlord kept raising the rent on us. It was so hard for us to find a rental because I'm young and Māori, and my partner is young as well. Eventually I said, "I've had enough, I'm going to buy a house."'

She said having that motivation to get out of the rental market got them under way. The house they were living in was mouldy and giving her asthma, yet the rent was about to increase from $450 to $500 a week without any remediation planned.

Sherman had been contributing to KiwiSaver since he was 15 and Shara since she started work. He had saved $39,000 and she had $10,000.

'We put our heads down, I worked any extra hours I could, he worked extra hours. He had $10,000 from car loans so the first thing we did was wipe all our debt. We did that and then we saved another $10,000. When we started looking for a mortgage broker we had $60,000.'

In total, it took them about two years to save their deposit and clear about $14,000 of debt.

Shara set a budget and realised they were spending more than they needed to. The couple were able to cut their spending by half. Shara forced herself to cut ties with Afterpay and Laybuy. 'At first it was hard for me to adjust, not being able to buy clothes . . . but it's just a couple of years of your life.'

It helped to tell people around them what they were doing, she said. 'We put up boundaries with friends and family. They all like to go out and do things so we told them what we were trying to do. Some people didn't think we could do it; we both worked at a supermarket and I was on student wages.'

Sherman says they wondered sometimes whether it would be possible, but they figured that even if they didn't manage to buy a house, they would still be in a better financial place because of the experience.

The couple took in boarders to help pay their rent, took on extra work where they could and tried to get as many things as possible either secondhand or free, to cut what they had to buy from the shops.

With their $60,000 deposit, a mortgage broker told them they could borrow $400,000. It was hard to find a property they liked in that budget so the broker suggested they look at a new build. That would give them an extra $10,000 from the First Home Grant to add to their deposit. 'We ended up getting $70,000 with those grants on top. If the money was there, we were going to use it.'

They bought a house and land package for $500,000.

'We were quite lucky. We had really good timing buying our house. Now that we know the process of buying we've helped others. It's very hard when you don't have any guidance or anyone around to help but now we know, we help a lot of our friends who are getting into the process. It can be quite confusing if you don't know what to do with lawyers and things like that,' Sherman says.

Their mortgage repayments have been cheaper than the rent they were paying previously, and Shara and Sherman haven't looked back.

'Why would you want to pay for someone else's holiday when you can pay for your own house?'

## How much deposit is enough?

If you are able to access a First Home Loan, you'll only need to have 5 per cent of the potential purchase price of your intended property to be able to qualify for a mortgage. For a $600,000 house, that is $30,000.

However, most people find they need to aim for a deposit of at least 10 per cent to get in the door of the main banks. This a good idea, not just because it makes banks more willing to lend to you, but also because it reduces the amount of time you might potentially have to pay a low-equity premium. It also gives you more of a buffer in case you find you have to sell your property unexpectedly.

To really clear your path to ownership, a 20 per cent deposit is ideal.

The Reserve Bank administers loan-to-value restrictions (called LVRs), which limit how much banks can lend to owner-occupiers who have less than a 20 per cent deposit or equity in any new lending deal. Investors have a different setting, which is usually set at a tougher level.

When the Reserve Bank's restrictions are tighter, trading banks are more limited in the number of low-deposit loans they can give out. From time to time, particularly if the rules are tightened for a period, banks stop all low-deposit lending on existing homes to anyone, to give them time to get safely back under the 'speed limit'.

But brokers say that even when times are tight, banks like to lend whatever they can to existing customers buying first homes.

McQueen says most of the people she deals with are aiming for a 10 per cent deposit, but if they can save 20 per cent, their options become much wider.

## Low-equity margins and fees

Buying a house with a small deposit can be expensive. You will usually be charged a low-equity premium until your equity gets to 20 per cent, and you're also unlikely to be able to access the best interest rates advertised by a bank. Banks usually reserve their best home loan specials for people with more than 20 per cent equity. You also probably won't get any cash back. ('Cash back' is the sweetener some banks offer to attract customers — usually $10,000.)

Then, on top of that, you'll often have to pay a low-equity margin or fee. This varies depending on how much equity you have. If you have between 15 and 20 per cent, you'll usually pay an extra 25 basis points to 30 basis points a year in interest, or a one-off fee that is added to the amount you have owing. If you have less than 5 per cent, you might have 150 basis points added. One basis point is 0.01 per cent, so a difference of 100 basis points could be the difference between paying 5 per cent a year and 6 per cent.

But as house prices increase over time, your equity will increase and you should be able to have the property revalued – or just rely on a desktop valuation if the increase across the market is sound – and move away from these extra rules.

## An exception to the rule

Even when the restrictions are tight, there are ways to get around them.

If you buy a new build, LVRs don't apply. This can be a good option for first-home buyers because sometimes it's cheaper to buy a home 'off the plans' (See page 153) and, if the market is on your side, you can pick up a bit of value and equity during the time it is being built.

Building is not as straightforward as buying an existing home, however, so it's important to understand what you're getting into, how long the build might take and how likely it is that you will face extra costs as the process goes along.

McLeod says he often sees people who have signed up to a new build living with their parents while their house is constructed. This saves them having to pay rent while also paying a mortgage on the house that is being built.

'You have to be careful and have your lawyer read your contract when you're buying new, but I still like it. You get a new home, plus an equity lift fairly quickly after it's built, which can be more comfortable. You might only have to wait a short period of time before you jump out of interest rates that have a margin on them. But the build can take anywhere from six to nine months.'

Non-bank lenders are also not captured by loan-to-value restrictions and many will offer home loans to people with smaller deposits. But if you choose to explore this route you will need to be prepared to pay a higher interest rate.

You can also ask family to act as guarantors to boost your equity. I will explain a bit more about how this works later on but McLeod says about 70 per cent of the deals he sees now involve some sort of parental input. Sometimes that's a small injection of cash to the deposit and sometimes it is a big chunk of money. He says anything from $20,000 to hundreds of thousands of dollars from family is 'normal'.

McLeod says people are often quite inventive with how they help their kids into properties. One family he worked with used the daughter's savings to subdivide a section that the parents already owned. This new bit of land would become hers.

McQueen says she often sees parents help their adult children to buy an investment property that the parents keep a stake in as well. 'That is because the parents themselves are not really on track for retirement and need to kill two birds with one stone.'

## *What's an LVR, anyway?*

*A loan-to-value ratio (LVR) is a measure of how much a bank is lending compared to the value of the property.*

*The Reserve Bank says that people who borrow with a ratio of more than 80 per cent – that is, they have less than 20 per cent of their own money in the deal – are often 'stretching their financial resources'. It reasons that they are also more vulnerable to an economic or financial shock, like a recession or increase in interest rates. It aims to protect them – but more importantly, shore up the stability of the financial system – by limiting how much lending can be made to people with small deposits.*

*Since 2013, the Reserve Bank has used LVR restrictions to limit how much of this low-deposit lending is happening, if it is concerned that it is creating a risk to the stability of the wider financial world.*

*If house prices are rising really fast, increasing the risk of a price fall in the future, the Reserve*

*Bank might tighten the LVRs to try to take some of the 'frothiness' out of the market and reduce the risk that highly indebted borrowers could end up in trouble.*

*The rules are usually tighter for investors than for owner-occupiers. Investor borrowing tends to be riskier because people are more likely to walk away from investment property in tough times while most people will do whatever they can to hold on to their homes.*

## A final note

McLeod says people going through the mortgage application process should understand they are not going to be told 'no, never'. They might just be told 'not now'.

More people are contacting mortgage advisers earlier in the process of buying, he says, to find out what they need to do to make buying a house possible, and to give themselves the best chance of getting a mortgage.

'Once you know what the path is – when the path becomes clear – it's more of a reality than a hope. If people want to build a deposit and get informed, they can understand how to set the goal properly so they can work towards it.'

## BUYER STORY:
## Helen

Helen bought her first home in Hamilton for $710,000 in October 2021.

She had separated from her husband three years earlier and initially took her son to live with her parents at their home.

'I left [the marriage] with $3000 but no debts, thankfully.'

She paid her parents board and saved everything she could beyond that, working as a nurse. 'I saved $70,000 in two-and-a-half years. I was into this goal and I was just going for it. My deposit was $130,000 and I borrowed $30,000 from my parents. The remainder was from KiwiSaver. I was fortunate that I had quite a good KiwiSaver balance.'

She said she was able to save the money mainly thanks to her parents' support. 'I had a really strict budget and because I knew it was for a finite period, I stuck to it. But if I had been renting there would have been no way to achieve it. I was saving $500 a week, I was allowed to spend $300 a fortnight on myself and I paid my parents $400 a fortnight for board. My salary was around $1700 or $1800 a fortnight – it varied because of shift work. I banked a minimum of $1000 a fortnight.'

If Helen didn't use all the $300 she set aside as spending money each fortnight, she would save that, too.

'The $300 included insurance, healthcare, any other food I wanted and childcare. I flew to New Plymouth a couple of times and went skiing once. I just tried to make sure that week to week I didn't spend money on little things.

'The little things are what add up, like going out for coffee. I had a small child and they are expensive in a different way, but you don't go out for dinner or lunch so much.'

She found the house she eventually bought after looking at about ten properties. It was owned by a trust that was interested in a quick sale. She made an offer with as few conditions as she could, relying on a family member who was a builder to do a virtual inspection rather than require a building report as part of her offer.

'Another offer came in half an hour before the deadline closed. I originally offered $690,000 and they put in their highest offer so I was told to put in my highest offer. I put it up to $710,000, which was as high as I was willing to pay for the place. We had similar offers but mine was accepted because I had fewer conditions.'

Helen said it was frustrating that banks were hesitant about lending to her because she was a solo parent.

'I used a broker but only one bank came back. I had a 20 per cent deposit and a good income, I have a good credit rating, no debt, and have never paid a bill late in my life. I had good savings and I was still seen as a high risk because I was a single income with a dependent.'

Chapter Three

# KEEPING IT IN THE FAMILY

Usually, as we get older, we rely on our parents a lot less (or at least we try to).

By the time you're ready to buy your own house, you might have lived away from your parents' home for a decade or more. It could be a long time since you asked them to foot the bill for anything.

But when it comes to buying property, many young people find that they need to turn to their parents to help get them in the door.

The 'bank of Mum and Dad' is a big part of the property market, and has been for at least a decade. Many of our parents' generation have built up good levels of equity in their homes, thanks to having owned them for a long time. They've paid off their mortgage and have benefited from a big run-up of prices.

Some people now suggest that whether your parents own a house can be a big determinant of whether you'll be able to do the same.

I don't subscribe to that view; I've seen lots of people whose parents don't own a home go on to buy a place of their own. But it is true that when your parents own a house, it can give you a lot more options when it comes to finding one of your own.

Brokers and financial advisers say it is becoming more and more common for first-home buyers to lean on their parents for support. That is particularly the case when lending rules are tight and banks need to see more equity in a deal.

When banks are more able to do low-deposit lending, fewer buyers require help. But when the rules are strict, buyers need every bit of help they can get.

It's been estimated that the 'bank of Mum and Dad' is the sixth-largest lender to first-home buyers. By some estimates, 60 to 70 per cent of first-time buyers now get parental assistance.

Consumer NZ says its research found that most parents helped by contributing to a deposit and that in 2022, the average amount of assistance given was $108,000. Sometimes that assistance is a bit of cash to help with a deposit, and other times parents are taking a share of a property or setting up a loan to their kids that is repaid alongside the mortgage.

There are a number of ways that parents can help kids into their first property. Understanding the options and how they work for both parties is really important before you get under way.

David Windler, a mortgage broker at The Mortgage Supply Co, says he recommends people start by looking at the gap that borrowers need to cover.

'Whether it's a single person or a couple borrowing, they have the ability to go only so far. We try to maximise the capacity of the "kids" to do what they need to do using KiwiSaver and their deposit, and then maximise their ability to borrow through their income. Then we are left with a gap – normally the gap is in the deposit.

'If we work out the kids' capacity to borrow through their income and know how much deposit they do have, we can measure how much parents need to put in [to cover the deposit shortfall].

'Then we can work out how much the parents need to be involved and limit their involvement to only what is needed and limit their risk.'

## Parents can act as guarantor

John Bolton, who founded mortgage-broking firm Squirrel, says a lot of first-home buyers are reluctant to ask their parents to act as guarantors on their loans and think of it as an option of last resort. He says, however, it's particularly common in times when the Reserve Bank's loan-to-value restrictions are stricter and people have to get to a 20 per cent deposit to have a chance of being able to buy.

While 'going guarantor' gets a bad rap and people will probably tell you terrible stories of parents ending up on the hook for all their kids' borrowing, including their kids' partners' ill-advised credit card purchases, most guarantees can now be set up in a way that limits the parents' exposure to the money that the kids need and doesn't put them on the hook for anything beyond that.

Most parents' lawyers are in favour of limiting the guarantee, but some banks do still like to see a guarantee for the full amount of the loan.

Bolton says it is usually possible to use a guarantee only for the portion of the deposit that the borrowers had not been able to save yet. 'If you're buying for $600,000 and you have a $60,000 deposit, the parents might guarantee the other $60,000 to reach a 20 per cent deposit.'

He says he usually moves first-home buyers to their parents' bank to set up the guarantee so the bank can easily access the security for the loan. This improves the borrowers' equity position for the deal and helps to meet the bank rules.

A limited guarantee on a parent's property would give borrowers a lot of advantages, he says. Borrowers might find it easier to borrow a bit more, can get better interest rates and go through an easier credit assessment. Basically, if they have their parents' backing, they can be treated like any borrower with a 25 per cent deposit. Banks sometimes go through phases where they only offer preapprovals to people with at least 20 per cent as a deposit.

Bolton says parents are often happy to help when they understand the financial difference their help will make to their children.

'When we show it can save your kid $20,000 over the next three years, they say, "Where do we sign?" The financial benefits are quite significant. If you're a first-home buyer with less than 20 per cent deposit, you might get a couple of thousand dollars cash [as a cashback]. But if you have 20 per cent you might get $6000, and the rates can be quite different. Some-times you get better pricing for a sub-80 per cent deal and in addition you don't have low-equity premiums and margins.'

He said someone with a 20 per cent deposit could end up paying a rate that was 100 basis points different from someone with a 10 per cent deposit.

'The difference could be as much as 1 per cent – and 1 per cent of a $600,000 loan, which is the average for a first-home buyer at the moment, is $6000 a year. That's $18,000 over three years. Parents want to help their kids but what gets them over the line is when they see the financial benefit it is going to create.'

Because having a guarantee is as good as having the deposit or equity yourself, you're in a much stronger position to negotiate. But it's important that a guarantor understands what they're signing. When someone offers a guarantee for a loan, even in a limited capacity, they are putting up their own security, usually their house, so the bank knows it has something to call on to have the loan repaid if the buyer fails to meet their obligations.

If the guarantee is limited, the guarantor is on the hook for a smaller amount, but unlimited guarantees can mean the parent ends up guaranteeing all the borrowers' loans, even personal borrowing and credit cards.

Parents usually have to prove they can service the borrowing, too, even if the plan is that they never get called upon to repay it. This can be a problem in cases where the parents are retired with a fixed income and limited reserves.

'Guarantees these days are income-tested,' Bolton says. 'That can sometimes get us unstuck if the parents are elderly or retired.'

It is essential that everyone involved in such transactions gets their own legal advice.

## *What's a guarantor, anyway?*

*Put simply, a guarantor is someone who guarantees that a loan will be paid.*

*If you don't have the security – in this case, the deposit in the deal – that the lender requires, it turns to someone else to provide that for you.*

*If you cannot pay your loan, the bank will then go to the guarantor to take care of it.*

## Subdividing

Sometimes people who have a house with a large section find they can carve off part of it to create a new property.

As the rules relax to allow higher-density housing developments around the country, this is becoming a more realistic option for a lot more homeowners.

One approach is for the new buyers to pay for the cost of the subdivision in return for having some land to build a house on.

This can substantially reduce the amount of money you need to build a home. Reserve Bank figures from the end of 2021 showed Auckland sections had a median sale price of just under $750,000, Christchurch $451,087 and Wellington $390,000.

How big a section needs to be to make this possible depends on the rules where you live. Your local council will be able to give you guidance.

If you cannot subdivide the section to create a property with a separate title, you might still be able to add a secondary dwelling on the section that could work as a short-term option while you save money, or longer-term if there's space.

Be aware that if your parents are doing this sort of thing for you with their property, and you have brothers or sisters, they may need to consider how this affects the distribution of their assets when they eventually die. If they've reduced the value of their property or their estate overall by helping you, and haven't done something similar for your siblings, they may need to amend their wills so that more of their estate goes to your brothers and sisters to keep things fair.

This is the sort of thing you can talk through with a lawyer.

## Buying together

It's possible to buy a house with your parents to get on to the property ladder – and for many parents, it can seem like a pretty good investment, too. They'll have guaranteed tenants – their kids – who they know will look after the place.

Buying together can give your parents some exposure to the capital gains the property should make over time and helps get you in the door. They can bring their equity and potentially their incomes to the deal, while you bring your earning power and possibly willingness to engage in some new-homeowner DIY.

But don't worry, it doesn't mean you have to have your parents move in as flatmates.

Here are a few ways you can make this work:
- You can band together, pool your deposit and have all your names on the title and the loan. You could make the loan repayments jointly, and plan to own the property for a set period of time, sell it, repay the outstanding mortgage and bank the capital gains to fund your solo house purchase in the future.
- You could set up a company or other entity to own the property between you, each making a set portion of the loan repayment. The first-home buyers could then rent the property from the company. The rent received would then offset all the owners' repayments equally.
- The first-home buyer could have full responsibility for the loan payments and the parents just provide the deposit.

Bolton says parents are often not keen to be named in the loan documents if the agreement is that they are only supplying the deposit. But banks generally require anyone who is on the title to also be up for a share of the loan.

A solution is for the first-home buyers to opt to hold their parents' share on a nominee basis so that they are the only people on the title and mortgage, with a legal agreement in place giving the parents a share of the potential upside of the property.

'A property-sharing agreement on a nominee basis is a good way of not being on the title and not having to be involved in the loan but having the protection of a legal agreement allowing you to participate in the upside of the property. It's hassle-free and a really nice, elegant way of doing it.'

Generally, first-home buyers do plan to buy their parents out at some point in the future if they plan to continue living in a co-owned home for a while. You'll need to decide how you'll work out what it will cost you to do that. Do your parents just want back what they put in, or do they want to have a percentage of the value of the property at the time you pay them back?

Your lawyer can help you draft an agreement at the outset that addresses all the questions that might arise. These might include questions like what happens if you decide you want to sell and your parents aren't keen, and what happens if the value of the property drops or if maintenance is required. It's good to know from the outset whether your parents are expecting to sign off on the paint colours.

If you're buying with a partner, a lawyer should also advise you on how to make sure that the portion from your parents does not become 'relationship property'. If they have given you a gift, your partner will become entitled to take half of it if you separate, unless you have an agreement clearly setting out what should happen.

There are also tax implications to consider if this will be a second property for your parents and there is a chance you might sell within the time limits of the brightline test, which means that tax will be applied to any profits you make if you sell within a set timeframe. Depending on how long you own the property together, they could end up having to pay income tax on any capital gains. Another good reason to get some expert advice.

## BUYER STORY:
## Sarah

Sarah had been checking Trade Me's property listings virtually every day for more than two years before the deal on her first home finally settled.

She was inspired to get into the market by her parents, who are now in their second home in Seatoun, Wellington. 'They are very aspirational and they worked hard for it,' she says. 'They are the only reason I even thought homeownership would be possible. Although they did get in without a deposit and consolidating their debts – unheard of today, it seems!'

At 23, Sarah was earning a pretty good salary working for the government and quickly progressed to $70,000 a year. She then started to look for a house in the outer Wellington region.

'My biggest mistake was not getting in then. Prices were half what they are now. But I was so keen to get there eventually. I knew my partner's family was going to sell a long-held family bach and that money would be used to help us with a deposit.'

She increased her KiwiSaver contributions to 10 per cent and started to pay attention to her debts.

'I had so much debt. Zero budgeting skills and way too high an income for my maturity level meant overspending and making credit cards and interest-free work for me. But I got my debts consolidated and just kept trying to pay them down as much as I could.'

But in the meantime Wellington prices had moved beyond her reach, so in early 2021 Sarah approached her boss to ask whether it would be possible to move to Christchurch while continuing to work in her job.

'They were very supportive and it was given the green light. So then we started visiting Christchurch and getting a feel for the different areas while we kept paying down debt.

'I started approaching advisers about our current situation and what steps we would need to take. They all said to try spending very cleanly and get the debt down or paid off. To be honest, we didn't listen or do well enough with that. In October, I moved to Christchurch and started flatting with a short-notice period so we could move into a home without a hassle – that's the luck of being young and not having kids. I moved into our preferred suburb, too.'

Sarah searched Google for mortgage brokers and lawyers who could help, and settled on a lawyer who offered a fixed price for conveyancing.

'It was really good to have some stability in our budget. We started talking to the mortgage adviser about what we needed to gather: bank records, proof of employment, address history, statements for all accounts. So many documents! It's very overwhelming.'

At that point, Sarah still had $25,000 in debt that she needed to pay off.

'I had been incredibly lucky in my career – shortly before moving to Christchurch I was promoted in the form of a secondment which had a really great salary.

'I was earning a base salary of $93,000 plus a higher duties allowance of $26,000. Annoyingly, the bank would only consider my base salary because the promotion is technically a fixed term. Although it was likely to continue, they can't take your word for it or gamble on an uncertainty.'

Sarah also had $27,000 in KiwiSaver and her partner's mother had promised $150,000 as a gift from the family property sale.

In the meantime her partner stayed in Wellington working and applying for jobs in Christchurch.

'He only worked part-time but he lived at home and saved every penny he could. He had about $7000 in the bank and he had no debts. However, he did have one default – well, we thought it was one at the time. It was an overdraft with ASB that had gone well overdue in 2020 with Covid pressures. It was $1000 but came to $1200 all up including late fees. We had paid it off in early 2021. Our adviser told us the one default should be fine and we gave a good explanation of what happened and how we could prevent it happening again.'

Feeling like she had a clearer idea of their finances, Sarah started going to open homes to understand the process before it was time to buy.

'I would follow houses I liked through the process and watch live auctions. I checked live auction results on real-estate websites each week to see what houses were selling for. I also started comparing that with the information on the OneRoof, Homes and QV websites to get a feel for the accuracy of their estimates. There was definitely a pattern in it but also some randomness that can just throw you.'

Sarah says she continued having Zoom calls with her broker to talk about the process and gathered more documents.

'Even though I had a great income on my own and we had a good deposit, we couldn't afford to borrow more than $400,000, which wasn't going to cut it for the suburbs we wanted to get into. Prices had jumped up so much in Christchurch and it was getting worse. So we had to get my partner a job. He had a few job offers come through in mid-November [2021] but they were all fixed term. One was permanent but it was a hazardous job he really didn't want. We talked to the adviser about the six-month fixed-term role and she said it would be up to the bank – they might not accept it but it's a case-by-case basis so we might be okay. Feeling a little threatened by rising prices, we just did it. He accepted the job and we submitted our application.'

The couple found a house they wanted to buy, which was going to be sold at auction. But as they were getting ready to bid, the bank discovered another default in her partner's name – unpaid fines from his time at university. Sarah was confident the fines could be overturned, but given the second default was combined with a fixed-term role, the bank said no.

'I wanted to keep figuring a way through but our adviser just seemed a bit uninterested at this point. I felt like she wasn't going to give us her best. She talked us through some other opinions and second-tier lenders but seemed reserved and thought we should wait to get the default wiped and for my partner to get a full-time job. But prices were going nuts and we knew we wouldn't be able to afford it soon (or even want it – I never wanted an $800,000-plus first home). So I started to do my own research into second-tier lenders and told the adviser we would not continue.'

At this point, Sarah gathered all the documents she had provided for the adviser and made a Google Drive folder, categorising them so they were easy to access. 'Then I wrote a letter outlining our goals, a summary of our current situation, and the amount we wanted to borrow and what we were looking to spend on a house. I included our employment history, our address history for the last three years, and our income. I then used the online quote tool for a few banks and if it seemed like a possibility, I emailed them with our letter.'

She contacted NZ Home Loans, which offers loans from Kiwibank and ASB, The Co-operative Bank and Resimac Home Loans NZ, who all replied to say there was a chance that the deal could be possible, so she sent over the Google Drive documents. (Of these, Resimac is the only one that is really a non-bank or second-tier lender. See page 112–113 for more about that.)

The couple made an offer on two homes but were unsuccessful. They then offered on a third, conditional on securing finance, knowing that it would help their chances of loan success if they could give the lenders a live deal to look at.

The Co-operative Bank said it would not be possible to progress the deal while Sarah's partner was on a fixed-term contract. Resimac said it couldn't help given the introduction of new, stricter responsible-lending rules that came into effect at this time (but which were softened slightly about six months later).

'NZ Home Loans were really upfront about that

new legislation. Basically, because our current rent and income did not equal our proposed mortgage repayments, we had no proof that we could pay a mortgage. Even though we had been paying equal amounts in personal loans without any missed repayments or issues. He said we would need to spend three months having the same amount each pay that the mortgage would cost, plus limit all our spending to the essentials.

'Luckily, we didn't get caught out by things like Uber Eats, but this was silly to us because we'd been paying loans and rent and saving above what a mortgage would cost. But paying off a personal loan in no way proves your reliability.'

The couple were left in a situation where a combined income of $190,000, and a deposit of $200,000 from KiwiSaver, inheritance and savings, could not get them a loan of $600,000.

'NZ Home Loans said to us that our income and deposit were clearly not an issue and that we could be borrowing a million dollars with that. But our lack of actual savings – not just a gift from Mum – and that proof of affordability (our spending and savings history) meant we couldn't even get accepted for half of what we could afford.'

Once NZ Home Loans turned them down, too, they asked their lawyers to cancel the contract for the house they had made a conditional offer on.

But then the agents came back to them and suggested a different mortgage broker who had been able to help other buyers get a loan.

'We really wanted to get into the market before we couldn't afford it at all. We'd long since ditched our preferred suburbs in Christchurch and started looking in Rolleston. But those prices were jumping up, too. So we approached the broker at Loan Market and sent him all of our documents. He said there was a chance but the interest would be high and there would be broker fees. We knew that if we just got into the house, the increase in value would balance out the extra we were paying and we knew we could afford it. So we asked the vendors for an extension to our contract – this is all happening a week before Christmas – and luckily they agreed.'

Sarah says the agent they were working with told them the letter they added with the offer about themselves and why they liked the house had made an impression on the vendors and made them want to give the couple a chance.

'So it was a slightly anxious holiday while we waited for our application to be processed. Sure enough, around 3 January the broker rang us and said we had verbal approval. It was such a relief. We waited for the conditional approval to come through – all they wanted was proof that one of the defaults had been paid. The interest rate would be 6.45 per cent [Reserve Bank data shows that standard one-year rates at this time were about 4.1 per cent] and we would have to pay the broker a fee of $6000 or 1 per cent of the loan. It was definitely a lot of money but I felt like it would be worth it. So we signed the agreement, sent the proof and waited for confirmation. Then we told the agent it was all go and wrote to our lawyers to say we could go unconditional.'

Sarah's broker ended up reducing their fee to $3000 and the process from then on was pretty standard, with an easy settlement.

'Since we first offered, the house has gone up in potential value by about $45,000 and the CV (capital value) has also gone up to $690,000 from $645,000. So we feel a bit secure in that respect – at least the CV is above the amount we borrowed.'

Sarah said it seemed unfair that banks weren't happy to see part of a buyer's deposit coming as a gift from parents.

'I just think it's crazy that people who have the means can't get a house. Or that if it's a gift from your parents, it's not favourable because you need to show you can save yourself. Who can realistically do that in this day and age? So many people rely on their parents' help because of crazy house prices and deposit requirements.'

## *A bank's view*

*ANZ is the country's biggest mortgage lender. It says there are a few things to consider and extra measures to put in place for the protection of both parties when you're thinking about using your family's help.*

*'Essentially there are four usual ways that parents can help out: by gifting money for a deposit; parents themselves providing a loan for a deposit; becoming a co-borrower; or providing security by way of a limited guarantee to reduce the LVR,' a spokesperson says.*

*When a gift is offered by parents, the bank would need confirmation, by way of a letter from the person giving the gift, saying that the money was given unconditionally and the first-home buyer would not need to repay it.*

*'If family members opt to act as a guarantor, we would calculate affordability for both the family member and the first-home buyer. The guarantor must be able to service the amount of the guarantee along with their existing financial commitments. We also set time frames which the guarantee must be in place for. Extra consideration is given when the parent is also guaranteeing siblings of the customer. We would need to ensure the guarantor*

*could service all commitments. We limit the total guarantee to a percentage of the fair market value of the family home.'*

*She says an informal loan can also be an option for family members wanting to help.*

*'We would need to consider whether the first-home buyer has to make repayments while they own the property and we would include any repayments in our affordability calculations. We would always advise that family members get independent legal advice if they go down either of these avenues.'*

## Family loan

John Bolton says one of the most common ways he sees people helping family members into homes is with a private loan.

If a couple separate after they have been given a home loan, it can be reclaimed from the first-home buyers. He says it provides a layer of security, especially if there is some disparity between how much each side is contributing.

'Parents can get their money back out,' Bolton says. 'You quite often see one side of the family putting in a big chunk of coin and the other not so much.'

Often a loan from family is basically a gift in all but name. No one expects it to be repaid and there is no interest rate applied, but it is structured as a loan to provide security and protect the contributing family member's interests in case things do not go to plan. Otherwise, repayment might only be required if the property is sold.

A lawyer can put an agreement in place detailing how much money is being lent and what the terms are for the loan to be repaid. Some families opt for zero interest or repayments unless a property is sold for a profit or the couple goes in separate directions.

Mortgage broker David Windler says this is often called a deed of acknowledgement of debt. 'Most of the time, to protect relationship property, the parents will give money to the child with a deed of acknowledgement of debt that says the contribution doesn't carry any interest cost and isn't repayable until the property is sold.

'That means we don't have to factor it in to the servicing calculations for the bank. The debt is repaid after the bank is paid when the property is sold and the bit that is left over after that is split between the owners.'

Glen McLeod says he would encourage people to borrow money against their home and then give it to kids with a deed of acknowledgement of debt instead of being a guarantor, because it avoids questions about the parents' ability to service the loan.

If a bank could see that the loan was clearly a debt and needed regular repayments, it might not qualify as part of the bank's calculation of equity in the deal.

## Gifting

Bolton has seen some people giving first-home buyers money as a way of giving them an early inheritance. Often this is the case with grandparents who want to help, he says.

Some people might sell an investment property and use the proceeds to assist with the deposit. This is the most straightforward way for family members to pitch in, but once the money goes to the buyers, there is no guaranteed way to reclaim it should something go wrong for the buyers or their ownership of the property.

## Specialised loan products

You might see banks offer products from time to time designed for family members to help first-home buyers purchase a property.

For example, Westpac offers a Family Springboard loan that helps people get a mortgage even if they only have a small deposit. It allows them to link up with family members either as co-borrowers or guarantors.

With a co-borrower structure there are two loans.

The first is a home loan in the buyer's name for up to 80 per cent of the value of the property. The second loan is shared with the other family members and is for up to 20 per cent of the purchase price, minus any deposit that the buyers can put into the deal.

The combined loans cover the purchase price of the property and the first-home buyers service them both, making repayments. If they are not able to make the payments, the co-borrower can be called on to pay them instead.

The liability for the family member reduces as the shared loan is repaid, and they get a say in things like the terms of the loan.

A guarantor structure, on the other hand, involves the buyer taking out a home loan for the property and the family member guaranteeing up to 20 per cent of its value (like the limited guarantee we talked about earlier). If the buyer cannot keep up with repayments, the family member might get a phone call asking them to step in and pay for their portion of the loan.

As is often the case with advertised products such as this, Bolton says most banks can offer something similar even if they do not have a loan product branded specifically to cater to this set-up.

It is also possible to have a family member's term deposit or other money in the bank offset against another person's mortgage, to reduce the interest cost and provide more security for the loan. This could be a good option for older people who have paid off their mortgages but don't like the idea of having any loans on their properties.

## Help doesn't have to be financial

If your parents are keen to help you get in the door of a house but don't have the money to give you a financial helping hand, there are other ways they can assist. This can be important if your parents don't own a house themselves.

One of the biggest non-financial ways that people can help family members is by allowing them to move in, rent-free, for a period of time. The first-home buyers can then save the money they would otherwise have spent on rent.

Another option is to have the would-be buyers pay board but then give it back to them when they are ready to buy a house, provided they have met their own savings goals.

Sometimes, if a parent owns a property but is low on cash, they might choose to sell part of their homes to their kids. This gives the parents some cash and the younger buyers an 'in' in the market, allowing them access to capital gains over the years that they could then potentially borrow against to fund another property.

This arrangement would require good legal advice to protect the interests of any other children who are not purchasing shares in the property.

## What if family help isn't an option?

Not everyone has family members who can help them into the property market.

Depending on your situation, you may be able to get into a house anyway with a shared ownership scheme. These schemes have been around in various iterations for a while, and can work well for people.

## Kāinga Ora First Home Partner scheme

For many people, the first option to consider is Kāinga Ora's First Home Partner shared ownership model. This is a government-backed ownership scheme that allows you to purchase a house with support from Kāinga Ora. You then buy Kāinga Ora out over time.

The biggest fishhook is that you must have a household income of no more than $130,000 as well as a good credit rating. You will also need to not have owned a house before, or to be in the same financial position as someone who hasn't. (These are basically the same rules as for KiwiSaver withdrawals.)

You will also need to commit to live in the house

for at least three years.

The maximum Kāinga Ora will contribute is the lower of 25 per cent of the purchase price of the house, or $200,000. You'll need to be able to contribute at least 5 per cent and meet the requirements of a bank to get a home loan to cover the rest.

When you have built up your own financial position, whether that is through saving, paying down the loan, building up equity through price rises or a mix of all of these, the amount you pay to own the house outright will depend on how much it has increased in value.

If the house's value has increased by 10 per cent, you have to pay back the amount the government initially contributed plus another 10 per cent.

After 15 years of joint ownership, if you have not bought out the Kāinga Ora share, you are charged an annual administration fee to cover 'reasonable costs'. You have to have purchased the Kāinga Ora share within 25 years from the day you purchased the property.

During the time that you own the home in partnership with the government, you have an annual meeting with a 'relationship manager' to help you work towards full ownership. You will also have to ask for permission to make improvements or renovations, or if you want to put your house on the market.

If you sell the house without buying Kāinga Ora

out, the sale proceeds are split proportionate to the share held by each party. If Kāinga Ora paid for 20 per cent of the house purchase price, it will get 20 per cent of the sale price.

## Private shared ownership schemes

If you don't meet the income test for a Kāinga Ora shared ownership arrangement, there are other options.

Some private schemes offer shared equity options for people who want some help into a house.

YouOwn is one of the more high-profile schemes at the time of writing. YouOwn buys houses with would-be purchasers as tenants in common (this is the ownership structure that allows you to have individual stakes in a house instead of jointly owning the whole thing).

The buyer is then responsible for all the rates and maintenance and pays a fee of 4.95 per cent a year on the money that YouOwn has invested in the property. Again, buyers need to have at least 5 per cent deposit.

There can be extra hurdles when it comes to owning with other people, whether that's the government or a private scheme, so it's important to talk to your lawyer about what you are agreeing to before you sign. Sorry if I sound a bit repetitive on this point but lawyers are your (expensive) friend when it comes to buying a house.

## Rent to buy

Every so often you might see houses advertised as 'rent to buy'. This tends to happen more during periods when the market is slower and developers are having a harder time getting the prices they want for their properties.

Rent-to-buy arrangements usually require people to pay more than market rent to build up money 'in' the property. At a specified date, or after a period of time has elapsed, or a certain amount has been saved, the tenant then has the option to buy the property, usually at a price that was agreed at the time the deal was entered into.

I've seen this work sometimes but have also seen occasions where households have ended up unable to complete the deal because they were still unable to qualify for a mortgage – sometimes they've been paying more than market rent (even with the 'saved' amount deducted) in a house that wasn't quite right for them in the hopes of a deal that wasn't going to happen. Depending on how tough the agreement is, they can sometimes end up forfeiting the extra bit that was meant to be 'buying' the house.

While private rent-to-buy deals need to be treated with care, you can also access the deals through not-for-profit organisations. One of the better-known rent-to-buy arrangements from a not-for-profit organisation is the Housing Foundation's HomeSaver programme.

HomeSaver is available to first-time buyers who have 'manageable' debt (that can be paid off within five years) and are on a household income of between $65,000 and $100,000 a year, although this can vary depending on which part of New Zealand you live in.

You get the right to live in the house for up to five years, with weekly rent payments based on what you can afford to pay but never more than market rent. After five years, the house is revalued and you get 25 per cent of the increase in value to use as a deposit. From there, you can either buy the house or move to a shared ownership arrangement.

If the house goes down in value, you have the option to rent until the market is on your side again.

## BUYER STORY:
## Laura

Laura says it wasn't as hard as you might think for her and her partner to buy their first house, in Ōtaki.

The couple went to a mortgage broker a few months before they thought they might start to look for a property and asked her to check their finances to see how well they were placed.

'She told us what we needed to do to get ourselves in the best position. We spent six months building up our cash deposit. I was pretty lucky I was able to do a lot of overtime through work so I could pick up some cash that way.'

Her parents were willing to help, too, and they decided that offering the couple a gift would be a better option than acting as guarantors.

'They looked at the guarantor option but found it was too difficult,' she says.

'We didn't realise that it ties them in as well. If they do that, they can't sell their house, there's a lot of limitations for them and that really wasn't fair on them so they ended up gifting us a small amount of money to help boost our deposit.'

The mortgage broker was able to get approval through ASB for a loan with a deposit of just over 10 per cent, and borrowing approved up to $580,000.

Laura says they started looking in Kāpiti but became disheartened when they found even small units were selling for $800,000 or $900,000. They shifted their search to Ōtaki instead.

'It's a bit further out but we can train in (to Wellington) and drive down. Once Transmission Gully opened it became a lot easier for us.'

They looked at a couple of houses – they missed out on the first house because an offer had been accepted before the open home. For the second, they knew they had to move fast.

'We went to the open home and decided we liked it so I contacted the real estate agent straight after we left and put in an offer that afternoon.'

Although Laura was worried that it might feel a bit cheesy, the couple also wrote a letter to the vendors of the house explaining they were first-home buyers looking to get into the market. 'It seemed to work for us.'

The offer was conditional on a valuation and within three hours it was accepted.

'We were really lucky. The main thing was to act fast. If we had sat on it and umm-ed and ahh-ed overnight someone else could have done the same thing and we would have lost out.'

She says people who are thinking about buying

should get their finances in order as early as they can.

'Budget. Banks do look at everything. Try not to get personal loans – even Afterpay can hold you back. And use a mortgage broker; ours made it so much easier for us.'

Chapter Four

# GETTING THE BANK TO SAY YES

For lots of first-home buyers, the most stressful part of the process isn't working out which house to buy, or how much to offer, or whether to get a building report or not.

It's the whole process of getting the bank to say 'yes' to lending what probably seems like a fairly crazy amount of money.

You've saved hard to get the deposit to get you started but now you need a bank to take you the rest of the way with a loan.

One of the first things you'll need to do is work out what kind of environment the banks are currently operating in.

A broker can give you a good steer on this. Sometimes, things are really tight, loan-to-value restrictions are tough and the banks are severely constrained in what they can do. Other times (2020, anyone?), the rules are pretty relaxed and the banks have a lot more freedom to give money to the borrowers they think look like a good bet.

When credit is tight – maybe the banks are only allowed to give a relatively small proportion of their new lending to borrowers with a small deposit – you might find it easier to get a loan after you have already had an offer accepted (conditional on finance, of course). When things are freer, you might be able to get a preapproval that gives you guidance that you can spend up to a certain amount and be relatively confident the bank will give you the money.

It's worth noting, though, that even if you have a preapproval, you should still make any deal conditional on finance because banks do like to check out the property they're funding before they send the money over.

To get that all-important 'yes', banks are usually looking for two things – that you have enough cash for a deposit to meet their requirements (or equity in the deal if you're pulling security in from elsewhere), and that you can afford to service the loan both now and potentially for the rest of the loan term. That could be about 30 years of your life – no big deal!

Here are some things you can do to boost your chances of success.

## Show your savings

When it comes to the deposit, lenders generally want to see that you have saved some of the money yourself.

You don't necessarily have to have scrimped and battled for the whole 20 per cent, but having saved at least 5 per cent of the purchase price by regularly putting money aside from your pay shows them that you know how to manage your money.

Even if you're getting a really chunky amount of money from your parents, the bank will want to see that you know how to do things like 'pay yourself first' and work towards a savings goal.

This proof of regular, intentional savings gives them more confidence that you are a good option and unlikely to fall behind on your repayments.

## Show you can afford it

Mortgage broker John Bolton says a good place to start when it comes to proving you can pay the loan is to start making the repayments now. He says that's what you need to prove you can afford it, and every dollar that you spend instead of saving is potentially going to make it harder for you to do so.

You can work out your likely loan repayments by taking the amount you think it will cost to buy the house, subtracting your deposit to get the loan amount you will need and then using an online mortgage calculator to work out what the repayments are likely to be.

Sorted has a great online calculator that allows you to check what repayments will be on various interest rates. Most bank websites also have a loan calculator.

For this exercise, you should use an interest rate that is higher than the rates the bank is advertising. That's because you may not be able to access the bank's specials, and the bank will apply its own higher test rate to the application anyway (more on that in a minute).

When the calculator spits out the likely repayment amount, you'll see what you have to start paying. If it's less than your current rent then you don't have to do anything – you're already showing you can meet the payments. But if it's more, start putting at least the difference into savings each week to show that it fits into your current budget and is manageable for you.

Adviser Glen McLeod explains: 'If you're paying rent of $700 a week at the moment and you're going for a mortgage that requires repayments at $1000, that's an extra $300 a week. Where is that in your spend? Have you got that left over? It might be that you don't, so the bank is going to ask where that money is coming from.'

You'll also need to leave room in your budget for things like rates and insurance maintenance. These aren't a problem when you're renting but will come at you quickly when you become a homeowner.

## Pay off your debt

Consumer debt is not your friend when you apply for a home loan. Lenders are going to raise their eyebrows if you send through an application that lists a lot of vehicle finance, hire purchases or other personal loans. (That doesn't mean you shouldn't disclose them if you have them – one of the quickest ways to get declined is to lie on your application.)

As well as being expensive to repay, consumer loans are an ongoing commitment that drains the amount of money you have available to pay your home loan. And having lots of these loans might make a bank wonder why you are turning to debt to fund your shopping, anyway.

You'll also probably need to cut back on your use of buy-now-pay-later platforms. During the crunchiest period of the banking rules brought in by the Credit Contracts and Consumer Finance Act in December 2021, borrowers were reporting that banks weren't happy about them having used the services at all, even if the purchases had been easily paid off.

These rules (which require banks to be more stringent about determining that people can afford the loans they take out) were tempered in the middle of 2022, and some of the brokers I spoke to were skeptical that one Afterpay would really ruin anyone's chances, but it's a good idea not to have a lot of different Afterpay and Laybuy payments flying out each fortnight.

Some of the buy-now-pay-later platforms allow you to work up to quite high spend limits, and banks generally assume in their calculations that you will max out your allocation. Cancelling your accounts for the time being is an easy way to clean up your finances and your mortgage application.

Apart from what the banks think of them, the platforms can make it a lot easier to spend more than you normally would if you were paying upfront with money you'd already saved.

Bolton advises that if you have the ability to pay off your student loan and consumer debt without taking your deposit below a key benchmark, like 10 or 20 per cent of the purchase price of a property, that can be a really good option.

'A student loan sucks up 12 per cent of every dollar you earn over the repayment threshold. If you're on $80,000 a year, that's roughly $600 a month, which would give you about $95,000 more in borrowing power.'

Even if repaying your other debt reduces your deposit from 18 per cent to 15 per cent, it's probably still a good move, he says. 'Anything between

10 per cent and 20 per cent is considered "low deposit" and the banks don't really mind which end of that scale you are at – they will treat all those applications pretty similarly.'

Bolton says that if you're comfortably over 10 per cent of the purchase price you intend to pay, but you don't have much hope of getting to 20 per cent before you buy, you could have more to gain if you pay off your debt and free up your income to cover larger home loan repayments.

## Ways to pay off debt

There are a few ways you can set about tackling your short-term debts:

### Snowball method
This is a great option for people who feel motivated by small wins and need positive reinforcement to stay on the path to success. Using this method, you focus your efforts on paying off your smallest debt first, while meeting the minimum payments required on the rest. Then, when that's gone, you move on to the next one. It's a good way to stay engaged through the process because you can celebrate each success. But because you're paying off the smallest debt, rather than the most expensive, it could mean you end up paying more in interest overall.

## Avalanche method

This is probably the cheapest way of paying off debt, because it tackles that problem. You focus on your most expensive loans first and get rid of those, then move down the scale. The sooner you get rid of those most expensive loans, the more money you save in interest costs.

## Never pay the minimum

If you only make the minimum debt repayment that's required, you'll take much longer than you should to get rid of what you owe and in many cases you'll also pay much more in interest than you should. Many hire-purchase agreements are set up so that they take longer than the interest-free period to pay off, if you stick to minimum repayments. Credit cards can keep you in an abysmal cycle of debt if you pay only the minimum required. Work out how much your budget will allow you to repay and work with that to create the best path to debt freedom.

## Check your habits

Generally, a bit of fun spending will not be a major problem for a bank unless it looks like you have a clear pattern of habitual behaviour.

Banks don't really mind the odd one-off big purchase in your bank accounts, but they start to be a bit wary about repeat activity or spending that you might find hard to stop.

One of the problems with the introduction of responsible lending rules in 2021 was that banks had less leeway to determine that someone would probably change their behaviour if their new home loan required them to, or if they hit financial straits and didn't have the money to keep spending as they were.

While the rules have been relaxed a bit since then, banks still notice anything significant that looks like it's going to keep happening. If you want to make your application stand out, it's best to avoid making any large amounts of frivolous spending a habit – at least during the months of account activity that you're going to show your bank!

Brokers say the banks are looking to see how your financial habits stack up.

'If I go through a client's spending and see a TAB payment, if it's $20 a week, that's fine,' McLeod says. 'No issue. But if it's $50 one week, $95 the next, $120, then it drops down, that's behaviour that shows a tendency to gamble, which, while it's not illegal, is something the banks are mindful of. It might be that for the next six months, you keep out of it.

'Buying coffees, dining out: these are all things that, if they are happening regularly, can be a problem,' he says. 'If you go out every Friday night and spend $200, that's regular spending. You might have heard people say, "I went and got a coffee and bought something from Kmart and was declined because of that," but the question is, are you doing that regularly?'

McLeod also advises shopping around for a better deal on your power and broadband to cut your monthly outgoing on those expenses, increase the amount of spare income you have available and make your application more appealing to a lender.

'What I do find when I do budgeting work with clients is the amount of money they spend on a monthly basis on takeaways, alcohol, dining out – people don't realise how much they spend doing those things. For some it's a lifestyle they will have to sacrifice if they want to make a move into property ownership.'

He says it's often not a change that has to stick forever. Once people are in the door of their own property and in the rhythm of home loan repayments, they can start working out how to reintroduce some of the things they enjoy into their budgets.

It's a good idea to close any credit cards you are not

using. Banks are required to take the full limit into consideration when considering your debt, not the actual balance you are holding on them. So if you have a $10,000 credit card limit but only $1000 charged up, the $10,000 will count against you in the application.

## *Test rates*

*I mentioned earlier that when you are running the numbers to see what you might have to repay, you should use an interest rate that is higher than the rates being advertised by banks.*

*That is because your application will be assessed against a 'test rate'. This will usually be a substantially higher interest rate that the banks use to determine whether a borrower could cope if interest rates rose. The lender isn't just assessing whether you can repay the mortgage for this year and next, it's potentially going to have you servicing the mortgage for up to 30 years. The test rate is sometimes two or three percentage points above the rates charged to retail borrowers.*

*The banks don't really talk about what servicing rates they are using but a mortgage broker can generally give you an indication.*

## Check your income

One of the biggest priorities for a lender is making sure that you have strong, secure income to keep making your repayments.

When lending criteria are tight, banks tend to give priority to existing clients who have the largest amount of disposable income left after their proposed mortgage repayments, brokers say.

If that means applying for a job that pays more than you are currently earning, it could be worth exploring. Or maybe it's time to start up a side hustle.

If you're in a fixed-term role, that can be bad news. McLeod says you normally need to be on at least a 12-month contract before a bank will be happy to lend to you. If you are self-employed you'll also need to be able to offer at least 12 months' worth of financial statements, and often two years' worth, to show what you are making.

It can be prudent to have a meeting with a mortgage adviser early in the process, so you can identify the weaknesses in your application and take steps to combat them. You'll get a good idea of what spending could be problematic and what you can reasonably aim for given your current settings.

## A bank's advice

*I asked the country's biggest bank what advice it can offer to people who want to apply for a home loan.*

*At the top of the list from ANZ was to check that you have 90 days' worth of bank statements for the account or accounts that you use to pay expenses from. This could include your credit cards. You'll want to do everything you can to make these three months look as solid as possible.*

*The next thing is to collect evidence of your income.*

*'If that's in your bank statements, that's perfect – otherwise we may need pay slips, employment contracts or other documents that show income,' a spokeswoman for ANZ says.*

*It's preferable to have these documents in an electronic format – a broker or lender will be able to advise what's best.*

*The ANZ spokeswoman says people should try to get to know roughly what they spend each month on food, utilities, travel and other things.*

*'Customers should have a think about what their current expenses are and how these could – or should – change after they receive the lending.'*

*The spokeswoman says customers should prepare for more in-depth questions about their finances. 'Customers who have a relationship with ANZ going back many years will be assessed using the same criteria as someone who is new to the bank.'*

## Non-bank lenders

Sometimes, if things don't quite work with a mainstream bank, you might choose to go to another lender for your finance.

This can be an option if your deal is slightly out of the ordinary or there is something about your criteria that doesn't fit what the banks are looking for. Sarah's case study (See pages 75–84) is a good example of this – her partner had a slightly dicey credit record and was employed on a fixed-term contract, which wasn't a great combo deal for the bank.

Some specialist non-bank lenders are set up to help people with poor credit or who are self-employed with income that is difficult to verify.

Brokers sometimes recommend that you stay with a lender like this for a while to build up some history (and hopefully some equity in your property) before trying to refinance with a bank.

Non-bank lenders generally charge a higher interest rate than the mainstream banks, but they are not governed by loan-to-value restrictions like the big banks. You do not have to think of this sort of lending as a permanent solution – it can just be a good stepping stone.

There are a few terms you might hear as you navigate the non-bank world.

## Near-prime

This is a term used to describe 'second-tier' lenders who sit just below the banks. They are slightly more expensive than a standard lender, but maybe not a whole lot once you take the banks' low-equity margins into account. Generally, these lenders pick up the sort of deals that 'almost' make it through at the mainstream banks. ('Prime' is used to describe high-quality borrowers who are usually snapped up by the banks.)

## Second or caveat lending

This type of lending is usually for small sums of money. It is designed to be used to improve your property's value, and then be repaid either through the sale of the property or the loan being refinanced. It's usually on top of an existing loan.

## Full doc

This is a loan that requires all the documentation that you'd expect to hand over to a bank. If you're going for a full-doc loan, you're expecting to give bank statements, proof of employment, credit card statements and more.

## Alt doc

This means that you're using other methods to prove your income and assets. This could be useful if you have the sort of income that wouldn't meet the requirements of a mainstream lender – perhaps a commission-only job without a clear track record, or maybe you've only been in business for a short time and don't have two years of financial statements.

## Low-doc

This is basically the same as alt-doc.

## No-doc

Here, a lender takes you at your word about what money you have coming in. All you have to do is declare that you can afford loan repayments. Usually this loan would be secured against a property, require a bigger-than-usual deposit and charge you a higher interest rate. New responsible lending rules make this sort of lending a bit harder to get.

## BUYER STORY:
## Jade

Jade and her husband never thought they would be able to buy a house, but they managed to get their first place, in Auckland's Māngere, when Jade was 41.

Jade says the adjustment to homeownership has brought significant benefits for her family, including a feeling of being much more settled.

'We are loving it. We feel secure,' she says. 'We have our kids at the local schools. That was always a real fear with renting, having to move. Being in our own family home has led to a lot more peace of mind. We get to decide when we go and where we go. Before, it was always in the back of our heads: don't get too settled.'

The couple bought their house in the first week of a Level 4 lockdown, in September 2021, but had been thinking about trying to buy a house since Christmas 2020.

'It started when I was complaining that I wanted a dishwasher, and we knew our landlord wouldn't put one in. We looked in our KiwiSavers and realised we had a little bit in there.'

They started working with Kāinga Ora with a view to buying through KiwiBuild, including going on a six-week course to understand the implications of buying a home.

But their applications for KiwiBuild were unsuccessful because there was so much competition for the homes that were available.

'It was up and down,' Jade says. 'We would get really hopeful and then it wouldn't go anywhere. So we started looking outside the KiwiBuild process and found a house we wanted. We had a lot of help from our parents – that was really good to help us get in.'

Jade's parents-in-law gave the couple a gift of some money that went towards their deposit and her own parents took out a reverse mortgage on their home to offer some money.

'That comes out of my inheritance when they eventually pass,' she says. 'Between the two amounts, we had more than a 20 per cent deposit, which made it really easy to get a loan.'

Buying during lockdown was a bit weird, she says. 'We'd only seen the place once. Our parents went through the next open home and we were planning to go back and look again but then the country closed down.

'It ended up being an online auction and my father-in-law bid for us on the phone. My father-in-law and mother-in-law are real estate agents and knew the auctioneer so we left it in my father-in-law's hands. He went a little higher than we wanted but it all worked out. The house fitted what we wanted.'

The townhouse, which Jade describes as 'nothing fancy' – 'It's nothing you'd call a dream house but it's everything we need' – sold under the hammer for $840,000. There was only one other bidder, who was also a first-home buyer. 'Everything came together for us.'

Jade says they used a mortgage broker her in-laws had worked with and followed their recommendations, including how to structure the loan. 'We thought homeownership was completely out of our reach for so long that we hadn't paid much attention to it.

'We took advice from people who do it every day. We had an easy process compared to lots of people. It was the first house we bid on, and it meets our needs. We went in thinking, "There are people who have been to 12 auctions before they find the place they buy," so we tried not to fall in love with it – even though we did.'

## BUYER STORY:
## Anna

Anna grew up the child of a single mother and remembers her family being supported by benefits through most of her childhood.

'Neither of my parents has ever owned a property. I became a solo parent at 20. I got my degree, had another baby on my own and moved into a really well-paying job that's super family-flexible.'

For the first two years, Anna earned $55,000, pro-rated for 25 hours a week, before moving up to $70,000 full-time in her third year. With Working for Families tax credits and some child support, her annual income is about $80,000.

Anna says she put 10 per cent of her pay into her KiwiSaver account when she started her job and was saving up as much extra cash elsewhere as she could, as well as paying off all her debt and buying a reliable vehicle.

'Once I'd saved 5 per cent for a First Home Loan deposit I met with the bank and they were happy to loan me around $400,000, which sadly priced me out of Nelson by a mile. And because I share custody I can't buy elsewhere and I can't use KiwiSaver for an investment property elsewhere while I rent here.'

She says she was also approved for the Kāinga Ora First Home Partner scheme but found it really difficult to navigate.

'They don't make it clear that it is for new properties only and they estimated Nelson prices at $600,000 for a new turn-key, but they were going for more like $950,000.'

Anna's investments took a hit due to Covid-19 but she managed to pull together about $25,000 in KiwiSaver, and $10,000 in exchange-traded funds, and had a gift from her grandmother of $20,000. 'I had a $55,000 deposit on my own, with a top-tax bracket income, and I still couldn't buy on my own in my home town.'

But she says she felt fortunate that she reached a stage with her new partner where he wanted to move in with her. He had bought his own first property with no deposit when he was 20 and had never had a student loan.

'He's bought and sold a few properties as an owner–occupier and built a house a while back. He's selling his current property in another town to move in with us. We have had an offer accepted on a home in Nelson, pending the sale of his place. We offered $890,000 on a 1960s home that was purchased seven years ago for $420,000.'

Anna says she felt aggrieved that even though

she had a good deposit, a high income and no bad debt, the only way she was able to buy a house was by partnering up with someone who could bring her deposit to 20 per cent of the purchase price, and with help from family.

'It's been quite straightforward so far. We have our finance with a mortgage broker who is doing most of it. She's taking her time getting back to us. We previously met with one to get preapproval in a situation where my partner was to keep his existing property. Despite having 41 per cent equity in it and a rental appraisal that showed he could rent it for much more than his mortgage, the bank wouldn't loan to us as we had less than a 20 per cent cash deposit.'

## How do kids fit into a mortgage application?

Back when our parents were buying houses, there was a traditional 'life process' that most people followed.

People would often marry, then buy a house, and then have children. But over the years, as people have started getting married and having their kids later in life, and houses have become too expensive for most young people to buy in the early years of their working lives, things have become a little less straightforward.

Now it is much more common to see people who have been together for a while, and who may already have a few children, thinking about trying to purchase a property.

The bad news is that banks are not huge fans of people with kids taking on large amounts of debt, unless you have really good incomes.

It is not that they don't like children (well, maybe some of them don't, but who knows?). In general, they're not keen on anything that sucks money out of first-home buyers' budgets on a long-term basis. And anyone who has kids knows that they can be quite expensive wee creatures for quite a long time.

Rupert Gough, who is chief executive of Mortgage Lab, says it comes back to what banks think of as the 'base cost' you have to cover each month, or the minimum your family has to be able to pay in expenses to stay afloat.

'If you live on white bread and rice and soy sauce and that sort of thing you can reduce your costs right down but the banks still have a minimum cost they use for each category.'

He said kids are another one of those categories. Even if a family is able to cut their costs – maybe by having really cheap childcare, for example – the bank will still add a minimum cost to its calculations that their budget will have to cover. He says that is usually about $500 a month as a minimum but will vary between the banks.

Gough says that means, all else being equal, a couple of first-home buyers who are applying for a loan and have children will have to earn $500 a month more after tax per child than someone who does not yet have kids.

'Costs go up for a couple with kids versus a couple without. The irony is that a couple with kids need more bedrooms so they probably need a more expensive house, but the bank has to take into account the additional costs. It's significantly harder for couples with kids. The $500 is after tax, so that couple has to earn $800 a month more.'

Any expenses you have for your kids may also be deemed to continue indefinitely, so you are better to apply for a loan after the subsidy for your childcare kicks in when the kids turn three, for example, than to try when they are two-and-a-half with the expectation things will soon become cheaper.

'One quirk of the CCCFA is that with the cost of education, whether public or private, if a child is Year 11 you've only got two or three years left of schooling but the bank still has to take that as an ongoing expense throughout the whole mortgage,' Gough says.

'That's often a frustration for people. Even if your child has only a few years left at school or [with a particular cost] the bank has to take it as if it's spread over 30 years. Whatever your expenses are now, even if you are about to get a subsidy, you've got to survive until that happens so the bank has to take it as it is now. The message is that the cost of having a child fluctuates depending on their age but the bank just takes your current expenses, and you have to take that on the chin.'

Gough says it's easier to get into the market before having kids as the bank doesn't query your expenses once the deal is done, unless you need to borrow more money. He says while people often wait until they have higher incomes, house prices also tend to rise over time, so waiting is not always the best financial option.

'You know what your expenses are when you own, whereas when you rent you are subject to the expenses of rent at that time. Once you have a mortgage the bank doesn't reassess unless you ask for more money. Having a child after you've got a mortgage, the bank isn't going to whip the loan away because you have an extra cost. It's up to the homeowner to think about how they're going to pay it [at that point].'

So if you have kids, what can you do? The advice for first-home buyers with kids is much the same as for any other buyer, except that you will have to prove that you can afford to cover the expenses of your family. Keep your spending as low as you can for the three to six months before you apply and boost your income as much as possible.

Run as much of a budget surplus as you can and be prepared for extra questions about what you spend on your children.

## BUYER STORY:
### Carrie

Carrie bought a home in July 2021 after renting in Wellington for a long time. She says she had a good set-up as a tenant, in a house out in Shelly Bay, which then became the site of a land dispute between a developer and occupiers protesting the development.

'I was living out there for seven years and then the occupation moved in and the developer kicked everyone out.'

Carrie initially lived there with her former partner and their two children, and says the rent was stable during her tenure. 'All the rent around town went up but that rent stayed the same. It was expensive when we moved in, for a three-bedroom house, but then everything else escalated. It was a cheap place to be living after the relationship broke down.'

She was given three months' notice and started looking for another place to rent for herself and two children, then aged nine and four, but couldn't find anything suitable. 'I didn't really feel like I was going to get any certainty out of renting in the area.'

She had $40,000 in her KiwiSaver and borrowed another $80,000 from her parents. 'They don't have a lot of money. That was their retirement fund – they don't own a house but they put it in and I bought a house in Whanganui. I couldn't buy in Wellington.'

Carrie says she was still owed a significant amount of money from the business that she owned with her former partner. Moving to a different town was an opportunity to leave some of the trauma behind and start afresh. 'Through all of that, the separation, I lost my job and I have been on the single parent benefit since then.

'Whanganui was a great escape for me.'

Initially, she says, she felt there was little hope of someone giving her a mortgage, but she spoke to a couple of mortgage brokers and started to think there could be a chance. 'I thought, "Hang on, I might be able to do this."'

Some mortgage advisers didn't seem interested in the 'curly circumstances' of her application, she says, but she was told that working through a broker would be a good option because they would speak to a number of providers on her behalf. 'I didn't find that to be the case at all. A lot didn't seem to view the benefit as income. I spoke to a few banks that were recommended to me as being a bit less risk-averse. None of them seemed that interested in me until Westpac said, "Why don't you go to your own bank?"'

'The mortgage brokers, when I was a single mum on a benefit trying to buy a house and living in Wellington, they didn't seem to want to know me. They didn't take the time to get to know my situation.'

Although Carrie had been given the impression that it was a long shot, she applied to Kiwibank, which she says was 'actually great'. 'They were over and above helpful, they genuinely wanted me to get a home. I don't know if it was because of my banking history or they were hungry for more business, but it felt more genuine and connected.

'I got a loan through them, and every day I wake up in this house and think, "I am so lucky." All the solo mothers I know in Wellington have to move from rental to rental every year and it's just horrific, it's so hard on the kids.'

The bank asked about her childcare costs and how much she spent on school uniforms but

Carrie was undeterred. She qualified for a Kāinga Ora First Home Grant of $5000 because the house was under the area's $400,000 price cap. 'I offered $415,000 and then negotiated down to be under the threshold because it needed some repairs.'

Carrie says it seemed to help that she was applying from Wellington, so the house prices in Whanganui seemed extremely affordable in contrast. The house she bought is a 1950s solid weatherboard home on a concrete pad, 'mostly identical to all the other houses on the street. I'm not sure if it was a state house but it has three bedrooms. There's nothing glamorous about it, it's not a fancy villa, it hasn't got beautiful wooden floors but it's incredibly functional and well built.'

Carrie says she had a feeling of desperation being stuck in an insecure housing situation. 'I'm 38, I've been through a traumatic time and I was wanting to provide that stability. What it's done for my mental health and getting back on my feet ... housing is a human right and it feels like we've lost our way in New Zealand. I'm one of the lucky ones and I feel unbelievably grateful.'

She and her former partner had been trying to buy a house in Wellington but kept missing out. 'We had been in the process of making offers on places and missing out by $30,000 so we'd have to go back to the bank and increase the amount we could borrow and shuffle things around to increase our loan and then the next house we put an offer on we would miss out by $30,000. It was constant scrabbling to buy a place. Luckily it didn't eventuate.'

Carrie fixed her mortgage for a period that runs until her youngest child goes to school. 'The bank recommended getting the fixed rate until she goes to school so I can increase my hours when I do work.'

She says the local community has been welcoming and there are other people moving into town from Auckland and Wellington. 'A lot of people are moving here so house prices are going up significantly. The locals seem really welcoming, although they're not happy about house prices going up! It's such a great town. Now I'm here and looking around thinking it would be nice to have a dishwasher ... I don't have the disposable income yet, I'm still looking for a job. The kids can walk to school and there are kids next door on both sides, it's really lovely. I couldn't have had that in Wellington in the area where my son went to school. The houses there are all over $1.2 million at the moment.'

## What if you're heading off on parental leave?

What better time to look for the house of your dreams than when you're on leave from work for 12 months (or more) looking after your kids?

The bad news is that while it's often a good time to plan for the future and get things sorted for your growing family, parental leave is not the period of your life when lenders will generally look upon you most favourably.

I talked to a couple who had built up a 57 per cent deposit for the house they wanted to buy but they were still turned away because the woman was only just heading back to work after a period on parental leave.

Even though you might have a solid job to return to, for the time being you have no employment income, which can be a problem.

The lender might worry that you will change your mind about going back, or that you might decide to return on fewer hours than you worked previously. You'll also have all those child-related expenses, which can be particularly crunchy in the first year after you come back from parental leave.

Broker Glen McLeod says that it's still possible to make an application for someone who is on parental leave if that person is part of a couple and – here's the tricky bit – the other person is earning enough to be able to service the loan by themselves. So you're all good to apply for a loan as long as your family didn't really need your income anyway!

'In most cases, it's a real struggle for someone on a single income to be able to purchase a home,' he says, 'unless, of course, they are on a really high income.'

He says the lender might consider both incomes if the person on parental leave was about to return to work and the settlement would happen after the first pay is received.

You'll need to be able to provide evidence that you've been with your current employer for longer than the past year, a letter from the employer detailing when you are coming back, and details of the salary you're coming back to.

If you're really stuck, you may be able to make the application more appealing to a lender by getting in a boarder or flatmate and including that income in your calculations.

## What happens to your mortgage if your circumstances change?

Kids are one of the main things that can really change your financial life and put you out of the workforce for a while, but they are not the only one.

There are lots of reasons why your money situation might change for a bit. You can insure against some of these scenarios – like getting sick and not being able to work. Talk to a financial adviser or insurer to work out what cover you need when you take out your loan.

But you can't insure against every scenario, so it's a good idea to have a vague plan in the back of your mind for how you would cope if something changed and made it harder for you to keep up with your home loan repayments.

Here are a few of the options that are typically available.

## Switch to 'interest-only' borrowing

You could apply to the bank to change your home loan to an 'interest-only' repayment structure. This means (as it says on the tin) that you only pay the interest part of your mortgage. This can be good if you want to reduce the amount of money going to mortgage repayments but it means you're only treading water.

The amount you owe does not decline. The biggest problem for most first-home buyers, though, is that in the early stages of your home loan, the interest part is the bulk of your repayment, anyway.

## Get a tenant

If your home has multiple bedrooms, you could consider renting one of them out to a tenant. Mortgage Lab's Rupert Gough says he is seeing more people putting a cabin or other secondary accommodation option in their gardens to rent out for a bit more income. This might not be ideal if your income has dropped because you've just had a baby but it can be a good way to get through other income shocks.

## Move out

This is quite a drastic solution, considering you probably bought a house in the first place so you wouldn't have to move out if you didn't want to. But if things were really tight you could move into a cheaper rental property for a while, or in with family, and rent your house out to give you a financial buffer.

## Take a mortgage holiday

If you know you're going to be without an income for a set period of time, you could apply for a mortgage holiday. This sounds great – who doesn't want a holiday? However, you're not actually getting a break from mortgage repayments. The bank just puts them on hold and the interest continues to accrue. This means you end up with a more expensive loan when you start paying again, or you extend the term and end up paying more that way. You usually have to go through the bank's hardship processes to apply for a mortgage holiday.

## Refinance

You could potentially save money by refixing your home loan. If you're on a term that has a while to go, you could look at breaking it to fix at a lower rate, or moving to another lender. This will usually have a fee attached but you can sometimes get a cash incentive to move to another bank, which can cover the cost, or if you're really stuck you can add the fee to your loan. If you have been paying off the loan for a while you could refinance it out to 30 years to reduce your payments, although this effectively means your journey to being mortgage-free starts all over again.

## Borrow

If you have owned the house for a while, you may be able to borrow against the equity to give you money to clear things like any credit card bills that are giving you headaches. If you do this, try to limit the term of the new borrowing. An extra $10,000 might not seem like much in the scheme of the loan but if you pay it back over 30 years, it can cost you more than another $10,000 in interest.

## Plan ahead

Gough says the best thing that people can do is to overpay their mortgages as much as possible while times are good, so that they are ahead on their repayments. That means if they run into problems, they have a buffer to fall back on. That, combined with building an emergency savings account with around three months' income stashed away, should mean they don't need to rely on any more drastic measures to cope.

## Making a hardship application

In the worst-case scenario, if you were truly struggling to make the payments on your mortgage, you might need to make a hardship application.

The Commerce Commission advises that the law requires lenders to consider applications from borrowers for changes to their mortgage if three conditions apply. Firstly, the borrower must have suffered a hardship they couldn't have seen coming (such as illness, injury or job loss), they have separated from a partner or a spouse has died. Secondly, they must not be able to meet their repayments because of this hardship. And lastly, the borrower must believe they will be able to meet their repayments if the loan contract was changed in a way that is allowed by the CCCF legislation.

You can get in touch with a lender at any time to talk about your lending options, but if you want to make a hardship application the lender is required to consider it and follow some legal processes. It's a good idea to talk to the bank as soon as you can see trouble coming.

You can make a hardship application at any time as long as you haven't been in default for two months or more, or for more than two weeks after receiving a Property Law Act notice (this is the kind of thing that comes your way if the lender is heading towards a mortgagee sale). You can only make one hardship application on the same grounds in a four-month period unless the lender agrees. But if you catch up, you can apply again.

Generally, lenders will do what they can to help

you get back on track with your mortgage because a mortgagee sale is not good for anyone.

When you make a hardship application, you can ask to extend the term of the loan and reduce the payments, or postpone the payments for a while (as per the mortgage holiday I mentioned earlier), or both these things at once.

If you have overdue debt and are really in strife and have fallen behind on payments you may also be able to ask your KiwiSaver provider for a withdrawal from your fund on hardship grounds. You can't withdraw KiwiSaver money for future mortgage repayments, even if you know it's going to be hard for you to pay them.

## BUYER STORY:
## Hannah

Hannah and her former husband decided to buy a house together despite having been separated for years.

She says they had shared custody of their children for nearly a decade. They were exhausted by the process of having them at one house for one week, then the other for the next.

'We had initially talked about finding houses

closer together but realised we couldn't both afford to buy. So then we started looking for houses where we could live as a family but where I could have a separate area,' she says.

'So then we were looking at places with granny flats, but it turns out that having a stand-alone dwelling on a property with a house is expensive, so we ended up with what we've got now — a three-bedroom house with an add-on done in the early-2000s, where I have a bedroom, bathroom and living area. It's connected to the main house but can be shut off, too.'

She says the unconventional arrangement is working really well.

'It was a total fluke we were able to do it. It was so out of our price range we didn't even look at it, but a friend knew the people who were selling and told us they would accept a lower price than what it was advertised for, so we took a look and ended up making an offer that we could afford.'

The deal required some extra legal advice to organise the structure correctly from the outset.

'We bought it as tenants in common rather than joint, and we made a relationship property agreement. We didn't have equal deposits but we treated it as if we'd paid 50 per cent each, and we each pay exactly half the mortgage, rates and insurance now.'

If they sell the house, they will split the gains in half.

She says the intention is to stay in the property for the long term.

'We bought it as the "family home" so we have no intention of selling any time soon. We also have the agreement that if one of us wants to sell and one wants to stay, then we buy each other out at market rates.'

Hannah says it's been good for the children. 'Each child has their own room for the first time, and one of them has literally painted murals all over her walls, which obviously could never happen when we were renting. It's perfect timing because they are teens now and desperately need their own space.'

She says the banks told them she and her ex weren't the only unorthodox couple they had helped into a house.

'They said it was becoming more common for people to buy as tenants in common and they'd seen more friends and siblings buying homes together. It all seemed routine to them.'

The former couple haven't had any major trouble living together again, she says. 'It definitely wouldn't work for everyone, though. And I do miss my quiet weeks sometimes.'

Chapter Five

# COULD YOUR FIRST HOME BE A NEW HOUSE?

For many people, the path to homeownership is through building a brand-new home. There are a number of incentives in KiwiSaver grants and loan-to-value rules that can make it really appealing.

Some first-home buyers buy from a builder offering a row of houses in a new subdivision, or buy an apartment off the plans in a brand-new complex.

Others strike out on their own and have a builder produce a dream home on a piece of land that has been carefully selected after the buyer has scoured the countryside for months. (This option is usually reserved for first-home buyers with significantly larger budgets.)

But, as with most property transactions, building

is not always straightforward. Unlike an existing home that you move into as soon as the deal is done, when you're buying a house that is still being built – or hasn't yet begun construction – you are putting a degree of trust and faith in the builder and developer to make it happen.

Here is what you need to know.

## Finance

In some ways, getting finance for a new build can be an easier prospect than for an existing home.

Loans for properties that are being built are exempt from loan-to-value restrictions, which means banks have more leeway when it comes to lending to people with deposits of less than 20 per cent.

You can also access twice the KiwiSaver First Home Grant (if you qualify, and if your new build is within the price restrictions).

Usually, developers will take a small deposit of between 5 per cent and 10 per cent of the final cost of the property when you sign up to buy, and hold that in their solicitor's trust account until the deal is settled and you have the keys.

Sometimes, apartment developers will take an even smaller amount of money to register your interest.

Holding the deposit in a solicitor's trust account gives you some protection in case something goes wrong during the development process. The developer can't just dip into your deposit to pay for an unexpected expense.

If you have a turn-key development (where construction of the property is completed before you purchase it), you do not pay anything more until the settlement date, when you are expected to pay the rest.

This is usually once a Code Compliance Certificate has been issued, but sometimes it's upon practical completion of construction – if your builder is aiming for the latter you will need to seek advice from your lawyer and bank about the implications.

This can be a big benefit to people who are saving hard. If you're in a rising market, you could also find that the property you are buying is worth quite a bit more by the time the project is finished and you are called on to settle the deal. Often, signing up to buy a property that is not yet built is cheaper than buying a comparable property that already exists, so some buyers aim to get instant equity this way.

But you'll need to be sure that you'll have the money available to you to settle the deal when the time comes.

Sometimes, delays with the construction process can mean your preapproval expires before you need the money. Buyers can sometimes face difficulties trying to find another lender to give them a loan, especially if their circumstances have changed – maybe they have a new job or have had to cut back on work for a while.

Property lawyer Joanna Pidgeon says this became more of a problem when Covid-19 caused problems with the supply chain for construction materials. Costs went up and delays added time.

'[Building new] gives purchasers an opportunity to lock in a price and keep saving with KiwiSaver and so on until you're ready to buy,' she says. 'Hopefully locking in a price and giving more time to save to get the 20 per cent deposit.'

But she says the experience of Covid-19 – creating lockdowns that held up building processes, pressure on supply chains making it hard to get materials, and staff absences at councils and Land Information NZ – showed how exposed buyers could be to delays.

'Finance can only be approved for a set period of time. With purchasers having to reapply for finance – life changes; people lose jobs, get pregnant – we have seen some people getting really stressed out, needing to settle before they go on maternity leave because they need to have finance approved. That is one of the problems some people are facing.'

Progress-payment-style deals differ in that you get a home loan approved for the whole cost of the project upfront, and the bank then pays it out in stages as the work progresses.

Usually that happens when the section is bought, when foundations are ready, when the framing is up and the roof goes on, and then when the project is complete.

The timing of the payments can vary but will be explained in any contract you sign. The benefit of this is that you have the finance in place from the outset, removing the risk you will be caught short and unable to settle. It does take a bit more management with the bank but these properties can sometimes be a little cheaper because you, rather than the developer, are carrying the holding costs.

## How long does it take to build a house?

There are a lot of things that can affect the time it takes for a property to be built.

In recent years, there have been major delays for things like plasterboard (such as GIB® board) and builders have sometimes had to wait months for their orders to be filled.

As a general rule, if a developer is building a lot of similar houses in one particular subdivision or development area, your house is likely to be built more quickly than a one-off, architecturally designed property that's being constructed on a specific piece of land among existing homes.

It's also faster if the services are all set up and

ready to be connected, and if the driveway is already in place.

But all sorts of things can make a build take longer – the weather, the type of site that is being built on (steep terrain can make it more complex and expensive), any legal process involved in clearing the site for your work to begin, any earthworks that have to happen to give you space to build on, and any vegetation that needs clearing.

Even things like public holidays can increase the amount of time you have to wait.

You should usually expect the build process to take about six months and the whole project to be anything up to a year. But factor in some leeway for delays and unexpected events to occur.

You will also need to consider where you'll live during the time your home is being built. If you can live with your family or a friend and save on rent, it could put you in a much better financial position when it comes time to settle and move in. Some people are able to save an extra chunk of money this way that can reduce the amount they need to borrow.

If you are paying rent and also making payments on a build process as it goes along, meaning you're servicing a loan too, it can put you under pressure. This is an issue for progress-payment construction contracts rather than turn-key ones.

If you are buying an apartment in a multi-unit

development, the construction period can be significantly longer.

## Choosing the right development

If you're going for a house-and-land package, or buying an apartment in a multi-unit development, there are usually a range of projects on the market to choose from. There has been a building boom in recent years and more homes are being built than at pretty much any time on record.

The right house for you will depend on a lot of things, including the location of the development, the price and the type of homes available. Some people are happy with smaller homes in a development closer to town. Others want a subdivision with bigger sections and don't care if it's a bit further from the CBD. Some people aren't fussed about carparks if the apartment is near a cycle lane, but others need a double garage.

Depending on where you are looking, you'll need to consider things like what amenities are nearby. When an area is going through significant development, it can sometimes be the case that supermarkets, libraries, restaurants and public transport are further away than you might be used to.

You will also need to talk to the developer about the quality of the build. What materials are being used?

What are the minimum dimensions of the property you are buying?

Sometimes plans make a unit seem a lot bigger than it will be in reality, so it is important to pin down the dimensions and how much usable space there will be in living areas.

If you are looking at a unit in a townhouse or apartment development, will there be sufficient soundproofing between the properties? While fences are said to make good neighbours in the suburbs, good soundproofing makes all the difference in high-density living situations.

Check what carparking you'll have access to. Some new builds have very little, which might be fine if you are happy to get around by public transport or other means. But it might not be so good if you are often ferrying kids to after-school activities in three different directions or you need to get to and from work at times of the night when public transport isn't running.

It's also a good time to check the reputation of the developer and find out what other projects they have been involved in.

Depending on the sort of place you are thinking about buying, you might also need to look at what body corporate arrangement could be in place when it is finished. These are the organisations that take care of the running of common areas in apartment buildings and townhouse complexes – but they can pop up anywhere there is shared land that is not managed by the council.

The body corporate will cover things like maintenance and building insurance if it is a multi-unit property, and can impose rules on things like the sort of pets you can have and even whether you can hang your washing on your balcony. The body corp will charge you an annual fee, which can add quite a bit to the cost of owning a property.

## What's in a title?

*One of the first things to do when you find a bit of land you want to build on is to find out whether the title has been issued.*

*The certificate of title is the legal document that explains who owns a property. It includes lots of important information such as the size of the land in question and any restrictions on how it can be used.*

*If a certificate of title hasn't yet been issued on the land, this is called untitled land and it means you can expect a few more delays. You'll need to wait for the title to be issued before you can apply for building consents, you will not have any services running to the section yet and you might have to think about access.*

*You could find the land is cheaper because of it, although it could be harder to get a mortgage approved until the title is in place. Sometimes developers who are planning a development will sell untitled land but then handle the process of getting the title for the buyers.*

## What could go wrong?

The big things that can go wrong with a new build are that the construction process takes longer than you expect, or is more expensive than either the builder or buyer expected, or that the finished product isn't what you were anticipating.

You can prepare yourself for such eventualities by allocating more budget to the build (lenders will usually allow you 10 per cent leeway) and expecting it to take longer than you hope.

While a new build might be a beautiful home with all the latest appliances and finishing touches, you also are not able to walk through it before you buy. Sometimes people find the finishes are not quite to the standard they expected or something is not as they imagined. Keeping really good lines of communication open with the builder through the process should reduce the risk of the finished product not being what you were imagining. Some buyers spend a lot of time dropping in on their new build to check!

A common issue for buyers, particularly in a hot market, is the use of a sunset clause.

Having a sunset clause in an agreement is not a bad thing in itself, and it can be really important to protect yourself if a build is dragging on beyond what is reasonable and you just want to get your money back and move on.

The clause gives you the opportunity to get out if things don't happen by a certain time.

But sometimes sunset clauses are also used by developers who want to resell the properties for a higher price.

Every so often you'll hear reports that developers have allegedly stalled on a project so they could invoke the clause and make the most of a market that has pushed up the price of the properties. They then ask for more money or sell to new buyers instead.

Not all sunset clauses apply to both the buyer and the seller, so it is worth making sure you know what yours says and what it means.

Joanna Pidgeon says sunset clauses have meant some people who thought they were signing up to a development have missed out.

There is no shortage of media reports of people who paid a deposit, thinking they were getting a good price, watched house prices rise over a year or two and then had the clause invoked on them. That sometimes means people not only don't get the place they were expecting but also find they are priced out of the market and can't afford another one.

'People thought they had got the property and through delays the vendor tips them out if the vendor can do it – or because of the delays and additional costs developers are seeking to get people to pay more to stay in,' Pidgeon says.

She says sunset clauses that are only for the benefit of the purchaser are much safer.

You will also need to know how much room the developer or builder has to come back and ask you to pay more money. If they can do so, you could face a bigger bill than you expect. If they can't, and the cost of materials rises faster than budgeted for, or something unexpected hits the supply chain (that's our mate Covid again), you could find the development stalls or they have to cut corners to get the build done. None of these is a great prospect.

Lots of things can affect the cost of a development, even once it's begun. There may be a need for unforeseen earthworks, there might be an increase in the cost of materials, there could be problems sourcing what is needed, or issues with labour, changes to the building plan, or buyers (including, possibly, you) wanting to add features that were not part of the original agreement.

Sometimes you can agree to cap the amount of price increase that you can cope with. Mortgage broker Bruce Patten says lenders usually expect a new build to run up to 10 per cent over the cost quoted at the outset. If you sign a house and land package deal and the land is worth $400,000 and the house $500,000, the bank will approve you up to $950,000 even if you are not (yet) expecting to spend that much.

Pidgeon says there are some ways that you can try to avoid delays. One is by considering how far the build has progressed at the time you sign up.

'If the developer doesn't have resource consent, doesn't have funding, or hasn't decided whether to proceed with the transaction, it's a lot more uncertain. There's probably also a bigger chance that it will be affected by delays and increases in cost,' she says.

You should also check what you are actually being sold. This might sound odd but sometimes the developer is selling the idea of a planned development rather than anything firm and that can mean, in some cases, that there will be long delays while the details are being worked out.

Sometimes developers look for expressions of interest before they have even secured the land to build on.

'If they're going to the market without even having

a price from a construction company, it's very difficult for them to price,' Pidgeon says.

'If margins are too tight, they might not be able to get finance because that lending to the developer will require a certain level of contingency before banks will fund the development.

'Knowing they have resource consent and are ready to go or have already started is usually a better prospect.'

She recommends researching the background of a builder or developer you're thinking about working with. What does Google have to say? Look at their track record, including their past developments, to get an idea of what your experience might be.

'How experienced are they? How professional are they? Look at their documentation. If it's sloppy with gaps it is probably giving you an indication they are not as professional as they could be,' Pidgeon says.

It's also worth thinking about what happens if the property market weakens during the time you are waiting for your build to finish. If you sign a contract to buy a property at a set price, you usually won't see that price drop even if prices fall in the wider market.

'You have to stress-test yourself. What might those different scenarios be?'

At the more serious end of the 'what could possibly go wrong' spectrum is the builder or developer going bust. This does happen from time to time. If the builder is a member of an organisation such as the Master Builders Association, they should offer you a guarantee – but it's important to make sure that the builder has done the paperwork to apply for this.

Check what rights any warranties or guarantees give you in the case of insolvency before you sign a contract.

If a developer goes into liquidation you could find the project is picked up by another company.

If things go really bad, depending on the type of business, you could become an unsecured creditor waiting for a portion of any payout. There's a chance that people in this situation receive no money back. Liquidators or creditors would put out information in this case that would tell you what to do to apply to be a creditor.

## House and land, or bespoke?

When people talk about buying off the plans, they are usually meaning a house and land development from a building company or part of a multi-unit development.

A house and land package is where you buy the land and the house build from the same company.

Usually there is a limited range of options to choose from, which makes things more affordable and scalable for the construction company.

It can make it easier to borrow because you are looking for funding for one amount rather than buying the section and then paying in instalments for the build.

The main drawback with these deals is that there are usually limitations on what can be built. The developments are sometimes on the outskirts of cities because there is not enough available land closer to the centre, and sections can be smaller in order to fit more homes in.

Buying a section and then building on it gives you a lot more freedom. You can choose the section you want and then find a builder who can put the house you want on it. You can have a lot more input into this sort of development but there is also a lot more potential for cost overruns and things not going exactly to plan.

If you are aiming to use your KiwiSaver to fund the purchase you will need to use it to buy the section because once you own the land you will not be able to raid your KiwiSaver to pay for the house. If you can pay for the house and the land at the same time you can avoid this problem.

## Builder guarantees

You do have rights if things aren't up to standard in your new property.

The Building Act has a 10-year implied warranty period, which applies whether it is cited explicitly in your contract or not.

It also gives you an automatic 12-month repair period from the time that your build is complete. As long as you give the builder or developer written notice of a problem within 12 months, the contractor is required to put it right within a reasonable amount of time.

This protection does not apply if the cause of the problem is beyond human control, or it was due to a third party's accident and the builder has no legal responsibility, or if you haven't followed the builder's advice, or if you've waited too long to raise a concern after it became apparent to you.

Consumer NZ says most problems can be solved through the negotiation process that should be set out in your building contract. It says you should seek legal advice if there is an issue that isn't fixed within a reasonable time – and you might be able to get someone in to fix it at the builder's cost. If the problem is so serious that the building is not safe, or it does not have the quality set out in the contract, Consumer NZ says the builder may have to pay you for the loss of value. As a last resort, you may also have the option of cancelling your contract – but it's a good idea to have your lawyer help you navigate that. Keeping really good lines of communication open with the builder through the process should reduce the risk of the finished product not being what you had hoped for.

## BUYER STORY:
### Jamie

Jamie says buying an apartment in Auckland was the best move she could have made to get into the housing market.

She bought a unit in a complex called Fabric of Onehunga and says it was the only way she would have been able to get into her first home.

'I bought really early, off the plans. I bought probably three-and-a-half years before I actually moved in. When you do that it's only a 10 per cent deposit and then you pay the rest on settlement.'

Jamie didn't use her KiwiSaver account to pay the 10 per cent and then worked hard to build up the balance in her fund while she waited for the apartment to be built. There was a delay of about six months or a year in the build process but this turned out to be a positive because it allowed her more time to save.

'I decided to keep building up my KiwiSaver for those three-and-a-half years until I moved in so I had more money to use and withdraw. It also meant that over those years, the apartment appreciated in value as well, so I now have a lot more equity.'

She says it is a good option for anyone who isn't in a rush to get into a property.

'There are risks, and design changes do happen, but if people are not in a hurry then it's such a great opportunity.'

She says the decision to buy the two-bedroom, two-bathroom unit was a bit spontaneous. A friend and her husband had done some research on different complexes being built and had bought a unit before she did. 'I have a couple of friends who have done the same thing. We're at the age now where fortunately a lot of my friends have houses but it's been through different routes.'

She bought the unit with the idea that she would rent out the second bedroom, but she has found she is enjoying living by herself.

The complex gives her an added feeling of security and she has a lot of friends among her neighbours.

'I never feel alone. There are so many lovely people here, it's a nice community. There needs to be a bit of a mindset shift from people needing a backyard to people living in a complex. We've made amazing friends. Even living by yourself, you never feel lonely and it's really safe. For me, it's not a forever home but I can see myself here for quite a few years.'

Some of the planned structure of the development changed through the build process, she says.

'It was meant to have floating walkways and an atrium and it was going to have a glass roof and the light would filter down the corridors, and internal windows. All that changed a bit, the design of the corridors changed, but otherwise I was really happy. It's a lovely development. Apartments here, when they come on the market, are only on sale for a few weeks.'

She says buying off the plans was worthwhile, despite the wait.

## BUYER STORY:
## Connor

Connor bought his first house in Tirau when he was 19.

He says being a homeowner has been a dream since he was 16 but it took hard work to get there.

'I worked really hard for two years. You've just got to say bye to the drinks at the weekends, the outings – I did countless numbers of 70-hour weeks and just knuckled down.'

The mechanic and his partner, who was also 19, saved a deposit of $100,000 for the new-build property, which was on the market for $750,000.

It has three bedrooms, two bathrooms and a double garage on an 800 square metre section.

Connor says the couple were renting a house a couple of streets over when they saw the development come on to the market. They managed to get a loan with a 15 per cent deposit and used money from their KiwiSaver accounts.

'It's been a dream of mine,' he says. 'I want to have my own place, my own freedom, to try to be independent.'

He says people who start young have the benefit of not having any dependents and can afford to save harder. 'You can really knuckle down and budget your wages.'

Connor was surprised at how fast house prices shot up through 2021. The couple put the deposit down for the property at the end of 2021 and within a month it was revalued as being worth $80,000 more.

Connor has lived in Karapiro most of his life but works in Matamata. He says Tirau is a good community, and there has been a lot of development and building in the area.

Building new opened up more options for the couple, including a better interest rate from the bank. Their loan was not subject to loan-to-value restrictions, which made the proposition more appealing to the bank. They were able to access ASB's 'back my build' rate, which at the time was 2.04 per cent, about half the normal retail rate.

'It's almost like building is the way to go now. You can get a lot of bang for your buck.'

He says he would recommend other buyers do what they can to get the most out of their KiwiSaver accounts. 'A growth fund is the best way to make your money work for you.'

Chapter Six

# THE SEARCH FOR YOUR FIRST HOME

You have your finances in order and you've worked out how much you can afford to spend.

Now comes the fun part. What sort of home do you want to buy?

You'll probably have people saying helpful yet deeply patronising things to you, like: 'Your first home shouldn't be your dream home.' As if you might otherwise have been planning to secure a nine-bedroom villa with an indoor swimming pool.

When you first start your search, the prospect of finding the right property from the thousands listed can feel daunting. How do you find the right one? What if the perfect one pops up the minute you go unconditional on one down the road?

There's no easy way to locate the right house for you but there are some ways you can narrow down the search a little.

## Apartment or house?

One of the first things many first-home buyers have to decide is whether they want to buy an apartment or townhouse, or a freestanding house.

Often, when you're looking at what you can buy for a typical first-home buyer budget, there will be a lot of apartments and units in your listings results, and some entry-level homes. To work out which is going to be the better option for you, you'll need to consider your circumstances.

Apartments can be great for a lot of reasons. They are often newly built with all the recent appliances and the conveniences that go with that.

They are often near public transport, or closer to town centres than free-standing houses.

There is minimal maintenance to be done on them by the homeowner – the body corporate will take care of most of the external work – and there is sometimes a community feel with others who live in the building or complex.

But on the downside, there can be problems with the building and it's important to do due diligence before you buy. You only need to look at the issues with leaky buildings over recent decades to see what can happen. To some extent, you are at the mercy of the other owners of apartments in the building when work needs to be done.

If you end up owning a unit in a building that needs a lot of maintenance or remediation done, you could find you are on the hook for a portion of a really big repair bill with limited influence on when that is due.

My advice is to be wary of apartments built around the turn of the century. In 2022, there were apartments still selling for less than people had paid for them in 2010, due to the remedial work required to bring them up to standard. If all you can afford is a suspiciously affordable apartment, you may be better off to keep renting.

If you're looking at an existing building, you can get some protection by reading the minutes of recent body corporate meetings to see what issues are being dealt with.

As noted earlier, you will probably pay a body corporate fee to cover things like maintenance of common areas and building insurance. The body corporate may also have rules that you have to abide by. You'll get a say in what the body corporate does but you'll be one vote of many.

Apartments tend to be smaller than houses, so you may find that you grow out of your property sooner, particularly if you have kids. You may be more limited in the cosmetic work you can do to improve the value of the apartment.

Generally, apartments increase in value more slowly than houses because much of the value of most properties is in the land component. When you own an apartment, you own a smaller chunk of the land the building sits on because it is shared between many dwellings.

Townhouses have some of the advantages of apartments – a communal feel, perhaps a body corporate – and potentially some of the disadvantages. Some townhouse developments, particularly in Auckland, have had weathertightness issues. But they can be a more affordable way to buy a bit more space than you would get in an apartment.

## Leasehold: Too good to be true?

*If you are looking at apartments or townhouse developments, particularly in central Auckland, you will probably discover some that appear amazingly affordable compared to their neighbours.*

*Often, these will turn out to be leasehold developments. (Or leaky buildings in need of remediation work and I encourage first-home buyers to stay well away from those.)*

*Leasehold properties do not own the land that the house or apartment sits on – they rent it from the owner of the land.*

*The rent can vary from not a lot – a couple of thousand a year, maybe – to tens of thousands of dollars. The problem is that the rent goes up with the value of the land, and if the area has gone through a period of rapid land appreciation, the owners of leasehold properties can be lumped with unmanageable increases in ground rent.*

*Sometimes you hear of people abandoning properties because they cannot afford the ground rent.*

*Generally, the people I've seen make leasehold properties work have been investors who could charge their tenants a high rent. If you are thinking about buying a leasehold property as a first-home buyer, it's important to get really good legal advice so you understand what you are signing up to.*

## Maybe you're after a house instead

Many people want to end up in a house of their own. If you can afford to buy a stand-alone property, that is the ideal for a lot of purchasers.

When you own a house, you have a lot of control

over what happens with it. Usually, no one sets rules for whether you can have pets or not (with the exception of some areas with protected wildlife that have covenants for pets, and your local council might step in if you have a menagerie that is disturbing the neighbours), and you can paint the house any colour you like, provided you're not in a subdivision with rules about house colours.

But many of New Zealand's houses are quite old and can have issues that you can't immediately see when you're walking through an open home. It's a good idea to get a builder to check out any house you're thinking about, to point out potential issues.

While rental properties are required to meet standards of heating and insulation, the same is not true of owner-occupied homes, so you may need to spend a bit of money on making your property warmer and drier, particularly if it's been around a few years.

You could find that for the same budget as an apartment, you're looking at a stand-alone house quite a lot further out of town, potentially without the same transport links that can make life easier in an apartment.

You're also on the hook for any repairs – external and internal – and you could have a lot of outdoor maintenance to do. You'll have to cover all the house and contents insurance and your rates will probably be higher than they would be in an apartment.

On the plus side, you should find that your property appreciates in value faster over time and you may even be able to put a secondary dwelling in the garden or add to the house if you need more space as your family grows.

## Small and close to the city, or bigger and further away?

Your next consideration is likely to be where you want to live.

In general, first-home buyers are looking at smaller properties closer to the centre, or bigger places further out in the suburbs, or even further afield. As an extreme example, at one stage recently prices lined up perfectly so a three-bedroom house I knew of in Birkenhead, on Auckland's North Shore, sold for exactly the same price as a 10-acre lifestyle block 30 minutes south of Whangārei.

There are clear benefits and drawbacks in most of these situations and what makes the best home for you will depend a lot on how you live. I know first-home buyers who were blissfully living on Auckland's West Coast beaches and would have happily stayed that way, working from home, except they started to resent the commute to take their kids into town for school and extracurricular activities.

If you have kids, you might value the prospect of a back garden for them to run around in enough to handle a commute that's a bit longer than normal. If you work from home, it could make sense to base yourself a bit further out of town to make the most of your flexibility and get more house for your dollar.

But if you have to travel into the office each day, or need to be zipping into town regularly, it might make sense to minimise your travel costs and buy as close to the centre of the city as you can afford.

It's hard to say what will be the best investment long-term. Generally, properties close to city centres appreciate in value in larger amounts than those further out. But higher-density properties do not always have that same growth and if you buy in an area where development takes off and there is a lot of infrastructure planned, you could find that your home quickly starts to be worth a lot more.

## Do-up or finished?

Many young buyers are told that they should look for the 'worst house in the best street' and try to do it up to add instant value.

There are lots of reasons why this can be a good strategy. Usually, location is a big part of what makes up the value of a property. If you can get a house in a good area for a better price because it's rundown, it might be a good move.

For buyers who have purchased with a small deposit, doing some work on a property and having it revalued can be a way to get closer to the 20 per cent threshold, when low-equity margins are lifted, giving you access to better interest rates.

But it's important to be realistic about the scale of the job you are taking on. A lot of older people in particular seem to imagine that all young first-home buyers have to do is pop to Bunnings for a couple of cans of paint to transform a house from dunger to amazing.

While you might see people adding tonnes of value with some pretty minor alterations in a booming market, doing the minimum and hoping for maximum returns is not a solid strategy most of the time. It is definitely feasible to build up 'sweat equity' in a property but it usually takes some hard work, or at least careful planning.

You'll need to determine at the outset whether the work required is cosmetic or structural and whether any of it needs to be done – or at least signed off – by a professional. Cosmetic work, like replastering walls, painting, recarpeting and even replacing kitchen cabinets, is the sort of thing that some people teach themselves to do.

Anything that involves moving plumbing fittings or making major changes to the structure of the house might need a council consent and professional oversight.

Get a good idea of the scale of the work before you begin and be realistic about your budget. I remember a builder telling me a bathroom renovation should cost about $3000. I knew that was too light considering we wanted to replace a shower and a bath. The job eventually cost us more like $30,000.

You also need to be realistic about how much time a renovation will require. If you're going to resent spending a lot of your weekends and evenings working on the house, it might not be a great idea. Similarly, if you have children who might not cope well with living on something resembling the set of *Extreme Makeover Home Edition* for months on end, you might think twice.

Consider, too, whether the market is right for the property you'll end up with. I once spent months and tens of thousands of dollars on renovations that didn't really add anything to the value of a property because it was not the sort of thing that made a difference to buyers. If you're only doing the renovations to make the house more enjoyable for you to live in, then go ahead and do whatever you like. But if you're doing the property up with the intention of selling and moving on at some point in the future, you'll need to also think about what future buyers might want.

There's no point pouring a lot of time and money into the house if it means you will have to sell it for much more than any of the neighbours' properties are worth to get a return on your investment.

And if you're in an area that attracts a lot of young families, you won't do yourself any favours if you convert a small bedroom into a bathroom/walk-in wardrobe set-up, as I saw one homeowner do.

On the other hand, buying new or recently upgraded means there are none of these concerns. You might pay a bit more but the work has been done for you and you don't have to set aside a renovation budget. You won't have to spend your spare time working out how to plaster a wall or polish a wooden floor.

If it's a new house, you can often choose your colours, fittings and fixtures and have it how you like it from the minute you take possession. If it's a house you plan to live in for a long time, anyway, you may not be worried about needing to add further value immediately.

## Local or somewhere else?

It has become common for first-time buyers, particularly people living in bigger centres, to think about buying a house in other parts of the country.

That is easy to understand when you scan the online property listings. What looks like a very average house in Auckland might be listed at $1 million while you can buy a five-bedroom house on a large section in Whanganui for less than that.

House prices in smaller centres have risen quickly but they are still less than the big cities, with the exception of the Queenstown Lakes area.

Sometimes, first-home buyers choose to buy a house in another centre and move there for a different lifestyle or different opportunities for their children.

Buying close to where you live now is easier in a lot of ways because you usually know the area pretty well. You'll have an idea before you start of what a typical house might sell for and what looks like good value. You know the local quirks and the sort of questions to ask an agent, what the local public transport is like, and you might have an idea of the local schools.

You can usually get to open homes at the last minute and visit a place multiple times if you want to check things before making an offer or bidding at auction.

Buying close to home allows you to hold on to your support networks – your ties to family and friends in the area – as well as retain your job. (Some buyers do find that their employer will let them take their work with them to their new homes, either remotely or in a different office.)

On the other hand, buying in a different centre can seem like you are getting a bargain. People coming from bigger centres are often surprised at how far their money stretches, and how close to the centre of a town they can live. Sometimes you might not spend a lot less, but you get a bigger house, more land, and maybe a more convenient location, for your money. You can arrange with real estate salespeople to look at a number of houses on a particular day if you are travelling in to look around an area. Both auctions and offer negotiations can be done online.

Many people who shift to a new area make use of social media groups and platforms like Neighbourly to get a sense of what's going on in the area and make some early connections.

## BUYER STORY: Suzanne

Suzanne moved from Auckland to Whangārei when she realised she and her husband could afford a better quality of life in the smaller city.

They bought a house for $800,000, which at that time was just under the median Auckland price.

In Whangārei, it bought them a four-bedroom, relatively new brick-and-tile house on a quarter-acre section.

'We had friends buying townhouses in South Auckland, commuting huge distances to work each day, for only a little less than we spent on our house in a really nice neighbourhood up here, where everything is nearby,' she says.

'My kids can walk to a great school nearby, the drive into the town centre is only about 10 minutes and the neighbours are great. Lots of them have moved from other places, too.'

Suzanne travels into Auckland for work when required but most of the time she works from her home office.

She says her only worry about the situation is that it could be hard for them to move back if they wanted to. Auckland house prices have tended to increase more quickly than Whangārei's and as time goes on it would be less feasible for the family to take a bigger loan to shift again.

But she says it's a problem she's happy to worry about if it ever comes to it. 'For now, I'm happy with where we are.'

Suzanne and her husband have also bought an investment property further north and rent it to a long-term tenant.

## Investment or place to live in?

If you like the idea of a house in a smaller, cheaper centre but you don't want to move there yourself, or you can't because of work, you might consider buying an investment property as your first home.

You could also consider buying an investment property in your own town or city if there are places there that are more affordable but not where you want to live yourself.

This helps you get on the property ladder and means you have a foothold in the market, often at a cheaper price than you would pay for an owner-occupied property.

You might be able to buy a block of flats in Southland, for example, for the same price as a house in an Auckland neighbourhood, and get a good rental return on the money invested.

This could be a good move if you want to own a property of some kind as soon as possible. You could sell it in future to fund buying your own home, or borrow against the equity you build in your investment property.

If you buy in a location where rents are solid, you could end up in a position where you have a tenant paying off the mortgage for you while you continue to live in your city and potentially save money for a future purchase, or enjoy the flexibility that renting the home you live in gives you. This can be really helpful for people who want to travel for work or don't want to be tied down in terms of where they live for now.

But there are some things you need to watch out for.

## KiwiSaver

If you withdraw money from your KiwiSaver account to buy a first home, you have to intend to live in the house for at least six months. If you receive a First Home Grant and don't live in it for that period of time, you can be required to pay it back, plus interest. If you use your KiwiSaver for the house purchase, it means you won't be able to use it in future when you buy an owner-occupied home. The KiwiSaver rules require you to be purchasing a property for the first time, or in the same financial position as a first-home buyer, in order to withdraw your money.

## Tax

Any investment property that you buy now will be subject to a brightline test. The Labour government increased this time-frame from five to 10 years in 2021 but the opposition National Party has promised to reverse this if elected in 2023. New builds were left at a five-year limit. If you sell a property within the brightline time period, the gains are added to your annual income for tax purposes. Depending on how much you make, you could end up paying 39 per cent tax on the profit of any sale.

If you live in a home for some of the period and rent it out for at least a year, the tax is applied proportionally depending on the amount of time it has been rented.

## Loans

It is a lot harder to get a loan as an investor than it is as a first-home buyer. While banks are often keen to help their customers to buy a property to live in, there is not always the same willingness to help you into an investor loan. The Reserve Bank's loan-to-value rules create a restriction, too. At the time of writing, banks could lend only 5 per cent of their new loans to investor borrowers with a deposit of less than 40 per cent, so if you are buying an investment as a first property you will need to have a 40 per cent deposit to put into the deal. Considering you can't tap KiwiSaver, this could be a big hurdle to overcome. You might end up having to look for very cheap investment properties, which can come with their own challenges, such as more maintenance, potentially tricky tenancies and limited potential for capital gains.

## Costs

There are a lot of costs that come with owning a rental property, particularly one in a different part of the country. If you're not living nearby, you'll probably need a property manager to keep an eye on the house, and you will need to budget for insurance, maintenance and rates. You'll also need to budget for occasional vacancies.

Investors used to be able to count their mortgage interest costs as an expense, which reduced the amount of tax they paid on the rental income they received. The Labour government started to phase this out over four years from 2022, although National has indicated it would reverse this, too. The rules have an exemption for new builds.

## Why are you buying?

If you are buying a property as an investment, you'll need to do the numbers and make sure that the property you are looking at works financially. While you can let your emotions interfere a bit when you are buying a home for your family, an investment needs to be more clearly a financial decision. If you are buying because you want to put down roots, an investment may not be the solution you are looking for.

## Forever home or stepping stone?

Traditional house-buying advice is to buy something small and then shift your way up to somewhere you want to stay for a long time.

That might have worked really well 30 years ago when house prices were cheaper and people were buying earlier in their lives. But with more people waiting until later in life to buy a house, it makes sense to try to find somewhere that you could imagine yourself staying for quite a while. Moving is usually stressful and expensive, after all.

The problem with finding something that is more like a 'forever home' as your first home is the price. If you're really squeezed, it might be easier if you find something that is a good option for now and focus on paying down the mortgage to set you up for another step in a few years.

But if you can stretch to afford a property that might be your home for a lot longer, it could make sense to do that rather than add a cheaper first step.

You will probably pay at least $30,000 in real estate commissions every time you sell, and legal fees will add thousands in most cases. While your forever home might always only be 20 per cent more expensive than your first home, in dollar terms that could mean a lot more money if house prices are rising.

In some ways you're better to buy as much house as you can afford as soon as you can get it sorted.

In 2007, I chose to buy an Auckland apartment for $315,000. In 2022, that was worth $730,000 according to homes.co.nz (the building did have major remedial issues, but that is another story). I also looked at a property on Tay Street, in Grey Lynn, which at the time was selling for $500,000. I decided I didn't want to take on the extra debt because at the time interest rates were near 9 per cent and climbing. Now that Tay Street house is worth about $2 million, according to homes.co.nz. That initial scary leap would have paid off handsomely.

## BUYER STORY:
## Jason

Jason says he bought his first house almost by accident.

He had a friend who was looking to sell a lifestyle block as part of a relationship break-up and was willing to take a relatively low offer to get out of the property.

He'd been told he wouldn't be able to get a home loan on his own because of some debt his company was carrying, but he and his partner were able to get a mortgage approved together.

The property was much bigger, both in terms of the size of the house and the land, than they really needed or wanted for their stage of life, but they saw it as a good opportunity to get into the market.

In the time they have owned the property, it has increased in value significantly and they are planning to sell to move to a property that is closer to both of their places of work.

'Working from home for some of the week cuts down our commuting time,' he says. 'But we still spend more time in our cars than we would like.'

# Chapter Seven

# LESS TRADITIONAL BUYING OPTIONS

Many people think of first-home buyers as a young couple or family starting out together and buying a house.

But life doesn't always work out that way and you might decide, rather than wait until you're one-half of a couple (if that's something you are aiming for), that you want to get into the property market in a different way.

This could mean buying with friends, buying with strangers, buying something other than a traditional property or maybe even investing in property via the sharemarket.

## Buying with friends

When prices are high compared to incomes, as they have been for decades, it can seem pretty much impossible to get into the property market as a single person.

For some people, this prompts them to consider getting together with friends who are in a similar situation to buy a place as a group.

There are lots of benefits to this – you can pool your deposit to have more equity in the deal than any of you would have on your own, you can split the mortgage repayments once you're in, you may have readymade flatmates who are also motivated to keep the house nice, and you can share the ongoing costs of ownership, such as rates and maintenance.

But things are not always totally smooth, particularly if you are in a situation where people have contributed uneven amounts, or have different expectations about how long you're going to own the property for.

It's really important to draw up an agreement with the help of a lawyer before you start the process.

The agreement should address things like:
- How much deposit each person is putting into the purchase.
- How the loan repayments will be split.
- How the sale proceeds will be distributed.

Will the gains be split evenly, or will they be proportionate to each person's contribution?

- How you will value non-financial input into the property, such as one person doing a lot of the maintenance work. If you own a house as part of a couple, you probably assume that you each pitch in and do things for the good of both of you, and it works out to be about even over time. But if you are a builder and find you are being called on by your co-owning flatmates to build a deck every weekend for a month, you might want a system in place to compensate you for that.
- Will you all live in the property? How will you cope with a situation where one person wants to move out and the others don't?
- What will you do if someone needs to sell and the others don't want to?
- How would you cope if one person lost their job or became too ill to work and couldn't afford the mortgage payments?
- What happens if someone dies?

Getting all this in writing at the outset can seem a bit like overkill. But it can save drama down the track and preserve friendships if a tricky situation does arise.

## BUYER STORY:
## Fiona

Fiona bought a house with a friend who had no fixed income but inherited a significant chunk of money. She herself had nothing saved but had a steady job so they used his money as a deposit and her income to prove they could service the mortgage.

The pair also got flatmates in and the bank that assessed their mortgage application used that income as part of its servicing calculations.

'We lived there as flatmates for a while, then I moved in with a partner and he had an extra flatmate for a while, then lived there with his partner and later their kids while I lived somewhere else.'

They had a property agreement that dictated that if either party wanted to sell, the other person would get first right of refusal. If they didn't want to buy the person out, the whole property would be sold and the money split according to contributions made.

While Fiona wasn't living in the property and a flatmate was taking her place, the flatmate's rent was counted as her contribution.

The property was eventually sold because her friend wanted to move away.

But the selling process was tricky, Fiona says. 'The main issue was that we hadn't altered our property-sharing agreement each time our circumstances changed, and decided how the income would be divvied up. So he assumed all the money he was paying for the mortgage and rates would be counted as his share [of contributions].'

Fiona had assumed that because he was living there with his partner and child, that half of his payments for the mortgage would have been counted as her share, because she had to live somewhere else.

They turned to an accountant, who went through the details and eventually it was decided they would split the proceeds 50/50, 'even though the accountant thought more should go to me since I didn't have the enjoyment of the property. But I was happy with the equal split as he had essentially operated like a property manager when I didn't live there, sorting out maintenance and finding flatmates. If we had held on to the property another year we would have got heaps more!'

Fiona was left with enough money to buy a car, have a deposit for a new house and do some renovations on her new property.

## Loans

Banks may be a bit more wary about lending to a group of friends than they would to a couple because there is a perception that things can go wrong more easily. But relationships aren't straightforward, either, and buying with friends is becoming a lot more common.

It used to be that it was possible to get a lender to allow you to mortgage each share of the property independently, with no obligation to pay a mortgage over the other owners' shares.

But broker Bruce Patten says the new responsible lending rules that came in as part of the CCCFA at the end of 2021 changed that.

'If you had, say, two friends buying together and both their names were on the title but they wanted a loan in John's name and another loan in Wendy's name, then each of them would have to provide a guarantee to one another.

'The problem this creates is that then each would have to show their ability to service the entire debt. Their debt, plus the guarantee portion. Often this doesn't work.

'We very rarely would take this approach. We would say okay, John, the -91 loan suffix for $400,000 is yours, but in joint names, and Wendy the -92 account suffix for $400,000 is yours, but in joint names.'

In this scenario, even if you have a joint mortgage,

many banks will set up the loan so you each have a portion that is paid out of your own bank account and you can determine what interest rate you want and how quickly you pay it off. That is useful if you are all paid at different times, or have different abilities to make repayments.

'That way each of them can choose to make payments at different levels, pay off lump sums, etc., and know it relates to their loan,' Patten says. 'We also suggest they draw something up with their lawyer that reflects this in case something happens and they need to sell or have a disagreement.'

You'll also need to remember that your credit-worthiness may be linked to your co-owners' ability to repay the loan. While your bank may set it up so that you each have your own payment to make, it is likely to still reflect on all of you if one of you falls behind or stops paying.

Owning a house with friends can also affect your ability to buy another property in future because the bank will count a portion of the house as your asset but will potentially take into account the whole mortgage as a liability.

You could also find you are liable for your co-owners' other debts to the bank, such as credit cards, so it is important to understand what you are agreeing to when you sign up for the loan.

You can also only claim a maximum of $10,000

in KiwiSaver First Home Grants, no matter how many buyers are involved in a purchase. You are also unlikely to remain below the combined income caps if there are a number of you buying.

People buying with friends usually purchase a house as 'tenants in common' rather than as joint owners. Some people set up a company to buy the house and then each hold shares in that company. (If you are planning to withdraw money from KiwiSaver to buy a house you may need to check that your KiwiSaver provider is happy with the house being owned in a company's name.)

Others even set up trusts to own shares in the company so that they can keep assets separate in case there's a claim on the property in future, such as someone having a relationship breakdown and their former partner claiming a share of the house.

The best structure for you will depend a lot on your circumstances so you should get personalised legal advice.

Some banks offer products that are specifically designed for this situation. For example, Kiwibank recently launched Co-Own, a product that allows people to combine savings with friends or family. It gives you the ability to share ongoing expenses like rates or maintenance and pool your resources to qualify for a home loan.

Most of the people I've talked to who have bought

houses with friends have found it was a good way into the property market, but only a short-term solution.

Many discover that before too long they were ready to move into a house with a partner and were thinking about having kids, which can be harder to do when you're living in a house full of friends (although some single mothers who live together with their kids seem to have life pretty sorted). But buying property should be thought of as a long-term decision because you can't be sure that the market will be on your side when it's time to move on.

## What does 'tenants in common' mean?

*Most of the time, when couples buy houses together, they do so with a joint tenancy and as joint owners. This means that if something should happen to one of them the property goes to the other. They don't own an individual share of the house, they own the whole thing together.*

*But as tenants in common, you have a specific share that belongs to you. It might be equal to that of the other owners or it might not. You can leave your share to whomever you like in the event of your death.*

# BUYER STORY:
## Sam

Sam has decided to buy a house in Auckland with a friend from university to reduce the deposit that he needs.

The pair are splitting the deposit requirement 50/50 and will sign a legal agreement that gives each of them them 50 per cent of the equity in the property when it comes time to sell.

'We're going to combine our capital and buy a place together. It's almost impossible to do so without it. It halves the deposit requirement on my behalf, he says.'

They are looking for a property in West Auckland up to $1.2 million. While it seems like a large price tag, Sam says a bigger and more expensive property is a better option because it allows them to bring in more flatmates to help with repayments.

'To have mortgage repayments that don't take up a huge chunk of your income you need flatmates. The price difference between three and four bedrooms is not that great but the difference in what has to come from your own salary is quite substantial. It pushes you to buy four or five bedrooms, so that there's us and then three flatmates on top. That's basically the only way you can keep mortgage payments somewhere shy of 50 per cent of your disposable income.

'The principal is a lot to borrow but buying at $800,000 and having only three bedrooms is not feasible. Buying at $1 million with four is, and $1.2 million and five bedrooms is actually more feasible.'

It's meant some negotiation with the bank – Sam works for ASB and has found that the bank will only take a certain number of flatmates and rent received into consideration when calculating what he can afford.

Sam has saved much of the deposit required in his KiwiSaver account but is also getting help from his parents.

'When I first walked into uni I set my KiwiSaver at 8 per cent back in 2016,' he says. 'When I came out of uni I had just shy of $10,000 in my KiwiSaver and that gave me a pretty good head start. I thought to myself if I walk into an entry-level job and set my KiwiSaver at 8 per cent I would never know if I was any poorer. I walked into a reasonably well-paying job out of uni – I put my KiwiSaver back to 3 per cent when I was saving for a car but then I bought a car and got a pretty substantial pay rise. I put my entire pay rise equivalent into KiwiSaver and bumped my contribution from 3 per cent to 10 per cent, which put me into a reasonable spot with my KiwiSaver balance.'

He says that buying a house makes sense.

'If you're not in it you're losing out. Rent is dead money, paying someone else's mortgage. Paying back a mortgage is almost like a savings account in a way because you're building equity and wealth. Property prices (usually) rise faster than incomes so the sooner you get in, the better. If you're not in it to win it, you're not winning at all.'

He says people who set their KiwiSaver contributions high from the start of their careers will never know the difference.

## Buying with family

You can use a similar structure to buy a house with family members.

As with friends, you'll need a good legal agreement because a potential falling out with family members can be even more fraught.

Anecdotally, I've heard of some people buying a share of their parents' home. This is often something that they expect to be passed down to them anyway, but owning it now means they can get more exposure to capital gains and the resulting equity to fund other purchases, and they could receive a bigger share of the proceeds when the property is eventually sold. This can also give the parents some money to live on if they are on a low, fixed income.

## Having others in to help

If you're not buying a house for your own family to live in with you, you might have more options in terms of who could help pay the bills.

You could buy a property with the intention of renting out part of it, either to a flatmate or in a short-term, Airbnb situation.

If you have a flatmate, you can set this up so the person is either a boarder or a flatmate.

Normally, a flatmate is not covered by the Residential Tenancies Act. But you can still choose to 'opt in' to the law by drawing up your own tenancy agreement in writing to describe how everyone is contracting in. You'll need to decide whether the whole Act or just certain sections apply. If you don't do this, then your flatmates don't have the rights – or obligations – that the law would normally give them.

A flatmate usually just pays for a room and then you split expenses as appropriate on top of that. In contrast, a boarder usually gets something else as well as a room, such as some meals or laundry.

The crucial difference, though, is that when you

have a boarder you don't have to pay tax on the income you get from them as long as it is less than the 'weekly standard cost' that the Inland Revenue sets each year.

Income from flatmates' rent is taxable, but you can claim your expenses against this. That means you can claim things like a portion of the power bill, internet and so on.

The tax deductibility changes I mentioned earlier mean that investors' ability to claim home loan interest costs against their rental income to reduce their tax bills is reducing over time. But in situations where you are renting out part of your main home, interest costs can still be claimed.

Robyn Walker, a tax partner at Deloitte, tells me that interest deductions will remain available in situations where you make part of your home available to other people, whether that is through having a flatmate, running a bed and breakfast or renting out part of your property on Airbnb.

'The rationale for this is to ensure that there remains an incentive to get in a flatmate,' she says.

'It's important to note that the house does need to be the "main home", so if the owner had flatmates and then moved out and retained the property as a rental, interest deductions would be unavailable from the time the property was no longer the main home of the owner.'

She says, in order to claim an interest deduction in the first instance, there needs to be a 'business' happening, such as earning money through rent. The interest is only deductible to the extent that the property is used by someone else. If a flatmate uses 30 per cent of your house, then you can claim 30 per cent of your home loan interest as a cost.

However, if a property has a separate, selfcontained unit or flat that you rent out then you are likely to be captured by the tax changes.

When assessing your mortgage application, a bank will consider potential flatmate or boarder income in its serviceability tests, but generally limits how much you can count on, usually to $150 or $200 a week. You may be able to get more in rent than this, of course, but the bank has to make sure that you aren't too reliant on an income stream that might not be sustainable.

## When things go wrong

When you mix family and money, it can become a bit tricky.

In one case heard by Financial Services Complaints Ltd (FSCL), which is a service that deals with complaints that cannot be resolved between a customer and their financial service provider, one family member was upset at how a mortgage adviser dealt with another family member's borrowing.

The man's father owned a property and wanted to free up money to do renovations, FSCL's case note says. FSCL doesn't identify the people who complain, nor the organisations they complain about.

He also wanted to have some money available to invest. He and his family decided that some of his children would purchase his house to give him access to that cash.

One of the sons asked a mortgage adviser to help find a loan of $300,000 to buy the property. But because he was self-employed and didn't have a good credit history, the adviser said it would be better if some of the other family members applied.

The only person who qualified for a loan was a sister. The adviser then recommended the other siblings set up a family trust that would protect everyone's interests.

But the man complained that the adviser had given bad advice and breached professional standards, suggesting the adviser had worked with the man's sister without anyone's knowledge, to allow her to buy the house on her own.

He said the adviser pressured him into accepting the arrangement once the loan was approved, and this meant his sister had the power to do what she wanted with the house. He said this had put him in a worse position because he was left paying rent to his sister and he wasn't happy with some of the renovations she wanted to do. He also claimed his sister stopped him accessing the house.

The man argued that the adviser should have suggested they apply to second-tier lenders, who might have been more willing to lend to other siblings as joint borrowers.

But FSCL rejected the complaint, saying the adviser had done what he was engaged to do.

FSCL chief executive Susan Taylor says people who borrow money with family should discuss and understand the terms of loans from the beginning.

'Not having these discussions early on can negatively impact the relationship later.'

## What if you're in a relationship with someone with kids?

Kids add weird complications to all sorts of things in life – and buying a house is just another one.

If you have a partner who has children from an earlier relationship (or you have your own) you might need to structure your purchase a bit differently.

That is because you might want to make sure that your children's interests are protected in case something unexpected happens.

In theory, if you own a house jointly, and then your partner dies, the whole property could pass to you and nothing would be left for their kids. (Or vice versa.)

Some people opt to be tenants in common if they want to keep their share separate. But it is also a good idea to get an agreement drawn up with a lawyer that dictates what should happen.

You can arrange it so that your partner could continue to live in the house after you died, while still protecting your share for your children.

If you are coming into the relationship with quite different financial positions, whether you have kids or not, you may also need to draw up an agreement that dictates how you want things to be split if you separate.

This is called a contracting-out agreement, and it can supersede the relationship property laws. Generally, if you don't have a contracting-out agreement, relationship assets like the family home will be split equally.

But if one of you brought a lot more money to the relationship, or covered a lot more of the repayments (and not because the other one was at home with children), you might want to have an agreement that sets out something other than a 50/50 split.

You will both need to get your own legal advice on this and it is a good idea to make sure that your agreements are kept up to date over the years. What seemed fair when you were starting out can be really outdated 10 or 20 years later.

## Buying through a property-sharing platform

You might have seen media coverage of platforms that offer to sell people a part of a house. This is particularly common when the market is running hot and people do not feel that they could afford to buy any sort of property on their own.

Buying together in this organised way is sometimes called fractional property ownership.

There have been a number of these schemes set up over the years, with varying degrees of success.

Generally, investors buy units or shares in a property. The property is then managed by a company, with rental income distributed to investors according to how many shares in the property they own, minus any costs (such as mortgage, maintenance, insurance, management fees). At the end of a set period, the property is sold and the proceeds are distributed among the investors.

Some platforms buy a house, while others in recent years have been land bankers offering investors the chance to buy a stake in land that they plan to hold for a period of time in the hope that its value increases.

These platforms can work in an environment where house prices are rising quickly. But if the market is soft, or going through a volatile patch at the time when you have agreed that you will sell, you may find the return is not so good. Owning a smaller proportion of a property also means you will only receive a small percentage of the profits, so you don't benefit as much as you would if you owned the house outright. I sometimes worry that opportunists spot a chance to gather investors who think they need to do something – anything – to get into the property market. You'll need to check that the investment prospects of anything you're signing up to are actually as good as you are being led to believe – and that you couldn't do better by yourself in a different vehicle.

You should also consider what you'd do if you needed to get your money back before the time the property was due to be sold. Many of these schemes are quite new and do not have secondary markets for people to sell their shares.

You will also need to understand that your returns and the cost of holding the property could change, particularly if interest rates increase more quickly than the rental return you are getting from the property.

## Investing in property via the sharemarket

Investors can get exposure to the property market via the sharemarket, too.

If you decide property is an asset class you really want to have investment exposure to, you could buy shares in a company like Kiwi Property Group, or Goodman Property Trust.

These sorts of investments will generally give you exposure to the commercial property market. Kiwi Property owns property like shopping malls, but other listed property companies own offices and industrial premises. It's worth doing a bit of digging to understand what these companies invest in because commercial property markets do not always follow the same cycles as residential markets.

Other companies, such as retirement village operators, have fortunes that are closely tied to the property market.

There are also property syndicates that buy commercial properties. These are a similar idea to the property-sharing platforms but on a grander and more expensive scale. You will usually need at least $50,000 to get in.

Property syndicates often invest in really big buildings. These can have good investment prospects but it is important to understand who might lease the property, whether there are any agreements already in place and how long the lease is likely to be for. Sometimes a custom-built industrial property can be empty for a long time if the tenant moves out or gets into financial trouble.

The Financial Markets Authority has issued advice on syndicates, and notes that some of them are building properties from scratch, which can be a high-risk activity. There are cases where investors have lost decent sums of money.

It also warns that syndicate managers do not have to return your money if you need it back but they might help you sell your share to another investor. That can come with fees attached and you might also end up selling them for less than you paid, particularly if the returns have dropped since you invested.

If you cannot sell your share to another investor you are probably stuck waiting until the property is sold, any loans that remain on it are repaid and the syndicate is wound up.

# (NON) BUYER STORY:
## Charlotte

Charlotte decided she'd had enough of being a tenant when she was given notice to move out of a property she had hoped would be a long-term home for herself and her son.

She had already planted fruit trees and become friends with the neighbours, but then the landlords separated and they needed the house back so that one of them could move into it.

She was tired of having to spend more than half of her income on rent, as well as dealing with regular inspections of her home, which she found intrusive.

So Charlotte decided to buy a bus and convert it into something they could live in. She wasn't planning to use it to travel around the country, just to live in as a cheaper housing option, with guaranteed tenure. She couldn't move somewhere cheaper than Wellington because her son's father was in the capital, as were her friends and her job.

The plan was to save enough money for a house deposit while living in the bus, which she first thought might take a year.

She borrowed $17,000, bought a vehicle and did the work on it to convert it into a livable home. Charlotte did most of the work on the bus herself, teaching herself DIY skills along the way. The process took six months and a friend allowed her to park her bus in her garden. She was working full-time throughout and would spend a couple of hours each evening on the renovation, looking up videos on YouTube as a guide.

The process of getting the bus ready meant thinking about every little detail. How would the lights work? How would she get reliable water?

Initially, Charlotte had planned to go without a shower in the bus, figuring they could shower elsewhere as it was only for 12 months. But when she realised that rising house prices could keep them there longer than she had expected, she decided a shower was worth the investment.

Some things about bus life have been harder than she expected, Charlotte says, like taking laundry to the laundromat or having to empty the toilet at a waste-dumping station. Things that you wouldn't have to worry about in a house have to be scheduled, like filling up the water tank and buying diesel for the air heater. She goes to the supermarket more often because there isn't a lot of storage space for groceries and in summer the bus was uncomfortably hot at times, driving them to friends with an air-conditioner.

But some things in the bus are easier, like cleaning and tidying.

'Sometimes I look around in amazement that I built this little home. I don't have skills exactly but I do have basic competence with so many new things and I have more confidence in general to give new things a go.

'We have everything we need: a bed each, light, warmth, a kitchen, toilet, wireless broadband, and space for clothes, books and other things. We have a couch to snuggle up and watch Netflix on and some plants to make it homely.'

Charlotte says the bus brought a sense of peace and relief because it gave her control over her living situation. 'If something breaks, I can fix it myself without waiting for a landlord who may or may not solve the problem. It's not an ideal situation but it is an improved one.'

When the market softened in 2022, Charlotte renewed her efforts to work towards buying a house and says she's optimistic that she might get to her goal before too long.

Chapter Eight

# REFINING YOUR OPEN-HOME STRATEGY, AND MAKING AN OFFER

Are you ready to get judgemental? Now is the time to go and look at houses and decide just how much you think they're worth.

When you've saved a decent deposit and are on your way to having your home loan sorted, you can start visiting open homes more seriously.

It's a good idea to start doing this earlier in the process, too, when everything is a bit more hypothetical, so you can get a sense of what open homes are like and how prices houses are priced in the current market.

But when things are starting to fall into place, it's

time to take your efforts up to another level.

You'll probably start by looking through every property listing you can find in your price range. There are a few things to think about to identify the sort of place that might suit you.

## The area

The suburb or even group of streets you're looking for a home in might be really important to you, maybe to retain connections to a network of friends, a local school, or your family. You might be willing to sacrifice other aspects of your wish list to get a place in the right area for you.

On the other hand, you might feel it's not hugely important to you exactly where you buy, as long as it's generally in the right area. Maybe you work remotely so you aren't stressed about a commute and you think the area is less important than the type of home you can afford to buy. You might check out school zones — even if you don't have children – because these zones can affect resale value.

For what it's worth, many investors recommend buying in areas where there is infrastructure development planned but not necessarily in place yet. If you can identify a part of your city, or another town, where there is significant money going into developing amenities, you will probably find this becomes a more desirable place to live over time. This isn't foolproof, however!

When you are thinking about an area you don't know very well yet, look at what's nearby. Not just things you need now but those you might want in the future, such as schools, shops, public transport and road and cycling connections. What's the housing mix like around you? Are there any developments planned for the area that could change it considerably? (Remember Waterview in Auckland before the tunnel and motorway connections went in?)

## Size of the house

Generally, the amount of house you will be able to get for your money will increase as you get further away from the city centre. Think about how you want to use the house, both now and in the future. If you work from home, you will need to make sure you have space to do that. You could consider the resale value of the property, too. A bigger house in the suburbs will generally, but not always, appeal to more families than a smaller one, so you could find it easier to sell when the time comes. But, on the other hand, there is usually less demand for two-bedroom homes, so you may find you face less competition if a smaller place suits your needs.

## Type of property

There are lots of reasons to choose different types of property. You might want an apartment so you can be at the centre of the action in a particular city or suburb, or you might want a lifestyle block so you can realise your dream of raising alpacas. There isn't a right or wrong answer to this but you'll want to compare properties of a similar type when you are doing your search so you get a good sense of what represents good value.

## Section size

Large sections can mean more competition from developers, which may push prices up. If you don't care about the potential for subdivision, or don't particularly want a garden, you might take your best shot if you aim for properties that are too small for people who want to turn one home into multiple dwellings.

## *Private sale*

*Every so often, you might come across a property advertised as a private sale. This means that it's being sold by the owner rather than via a real estate salesperson. As the buyer, this doesn't change a lot, except that you'll have to negotiate with the owner directly (which can be awkward if one of your reasons for a lower offer is that the decor is hideous). Banks may also ask for a valuation by a registered valuer to check that the price the private seller is asking is reasonable. The private seller still has an obligation to tell you anything that could be relevant about the property.*

## Price range

If a house you like the look of doesn't have a listed price, you can contact the salesperson and ask for a price guide. They need to give you a realistic idea of what a property might sell for, even if they're not sure of the exact amount that will secure it.

## Attending an open home

Some properties will have open home times and dates listed while others will require you to set up an appointment to view. If you don't have kids in tow, it could be reasonable to stack up a day in the weekend with open homes, maybe with a stop for coffee in between. But if you have small kids with you, it is likely that everyone will be happier if you limit the number of places you view to two or three a day at a maximum. There's nothing quite like a bored two-year-old to help you identify a property's safety hazards.

When you arrive, it helps to have a clear idea of what you are looking for. When you get out of the car, have a look around. What does the neighbourhood feel like? Is there parking on the street, if that's important to you? Does it seem like the sort of place that would be quiet, or is it a busy thoroughfare?

When you are inside, take your time looking around and ask the salesperson lots of questions. If the property has been staged (where hired furniture is put in place to show what a house might look like) check that the suggested set-up would actually work. I know of one house that had a sunroom set up as an office with a computer and desk in the corner. But the room had no power anywhere in it, so it would not have worked as an office in reality.

Real estate salespeople need to tell you upfront if

there are any problems with a property. Some people recommend asking questions over email, so you have a record of answers to things like: 'What do I need to know about this property?', 'Why is the owner selling?', 'Are there any things I should know about the neigbourhood?', 'Is this a leaky home?' or 'Have you had any offers and why didn't they progress?'. This last one might highlight something like a major issue in a building report that you will need to be prepared for.

If you like a place, you should feel comfortable asking to come back and see what it is like at different times. For example, a property next to a daycare might feel quite different on a Saturday than at 7.30 a.m. on a Friday.

## Your open-home checklist

- ☐ What kind of material is the house built from?
- ☐ Does it appear to be well-maintained?
- ☐ Are the gutters sound?
- ☐ Are the eaves clean? What's the condition of the roof? Are there any holes?
- ☐ Does it have sufficient bedrooms for your needs?
- ☐ How much storage is there?
- ☐ Is there space for your car (if you have one)?
- ☐ What's the water pressure like?
- ☐ If you put a marble on the floor, does it roll away from you? (This could indicate issues with the foundations or piles.)
- ☐ Check under the house if it's accessible. Are the piles in good condition (if the house has them) and does it look dry?
- ☐ Are any communal spaces clean and well kept?
- ☐ Are there any damp patches on the carpet?
- ☐ Are the curtains or ceiling mouldy?
- ☐ Does it smell clean and fresh, or is there a hint of damp in the air?
- ☐ Is the house insulated, and if so, is it still in good condition? (Insulation can break down over time.)
- ☐ How's the ventilation? Do extractor fans vent to the outside?
- ☐ How is the house currently heated?
- ☐ Do all the doors fit properly?

# Refining your open-home strategy, and making an offer

- [ ] What condition is the carpet in?
- [ ] What's included as part of the chattels? Are the curtains staying?
- [ ] Does everything work? Can you open all the windows and use all the power points?
- [ ] Do the toilets flush? (Yes, really.)
- [ ] What is the condition of the garden? Does the lawn seem boggy?
- [ ] Are there retaining walls that need fixing?
- [ ] Is there a body corporate? Can you talk to the president?
- [ ] Is the layout going to work for your family? If you have little kids, can you imagine being able to keep an eye on them from the kitchen if you're preparing dinner?
- [ ] Are the bedrooms big enough? Could you fit all your things?
- [ ] Will the wardrobes work for you?
- [ ] If the house has been renovated, are there appropriate consents in place for this?
- [ ] Find out from the salesperson how offers have to be made and by when.
- [ ] If there are things like a pool or spa, what condition are they in? Is any extra investment required?
- [ ] Where does the natural light come from?

## When you find the right one

You might get a 'this is the one' feeling and fall madly in love with a house. But you also might find that you just end up deciding on one that ticks enough boxes, fits in your budget and will work for now.

Both scenarios are totally fine. In fact, if you're not emotionally invested, you might find it easier to drive a good deal on a house because you won't be so alarmed at the prospect of walking away if it doesn't work out.

Provided the house is listed with a set price, or for 'offers over' or 'by negotiation', the next thing to do is to decide to make an offer.

The first step you'll need to take is to get in touch with the real estate salesperson, if there is one, or the seller if it is a private sale. The salesperson will usually come to you with a sale and purchase agreement ready to fill out.

Sometimes, they'll ask you on the phone what you are planning to offer and sometimes they'll leave the conversation until your in-person meeting. Be prepared for them to put pressure on you to increase your offer as high as possible. That's because they work for the seller and it is their job to get the best sale price possible.

They will usually say things like, 'If you missed out by $5000, how would you feel?'

The problem with this strategy is that you could keep going up in $5000 increments forever and end up spending a lot more than you intended. Be clear about what you are offering. Back it up with clear reasons if that helps you stand your ground.

You can give yourself a little room to negotiate by offering slightly below your maximum, but you'll need to be careful with this strategy if you are in a multi-offer scenario.

You can ask the salesperson for an indication of what the seller would accept but they are required to present all written offers. Many see even a low offer as a way to start a negotiation process with a buyer.

(People who are trying to drive a hard bargain sometimes talk about this requirement to present all offers as a win for them but I'm not so sure it's that clear-cut. There's nothing to stop a salesperson advising against a particularly low offer, and if you go in with one that is ridiculous it can put a vendor off being willing to look at another offer from you in the future.)

If a property is listed with a price, or 'buyer enquiry over', this has to be an amount that the vendor would seriously consider accepting. (If a property is listed with a price that's lower than the price the vendor wants, this is called 'bait pricing' and is not allowed.)

## What's a multi-offer scenario?

Bluntly, a multi-offer scenario is a salesperson's dream. It happens when two people are thinking about putting in an offer at the same time. Agents love this because it gives them the chance to pull the best possible offers from the buyers.

To qualify, there must be more than one offer in writing being presented to the vendor. The salesperson is allowed to hold on to your written offer and check with other people who were interested in the property to see if they, too, want to make an offer – creating a multi-offer scenario. That could include people who were interested in the property but have already had an offer turned down.

If you were first with your offer, the salesperson will come back to you and ask whether you want to review it, given that you now have competition. They'll urge you to put in the best offer you can and you really do need to do this because you won't always get another shot.

You'll also have to sign a form acknowledging that you understand a multi-offer scenario is under way.

If another buyer pulls out before the offers are presented, leaving just your offer, the salesperson should also tell you this and give you a chance to review your offer before it is presented.

The salesperson will then present all the offers to

the vendor, who will select one they want to accept, or will choose to 'work with' some of the buyers to try to get to a level that will see the deal signed.

They can choose to work with one buyer and not the others, or negotiate with everyone.

Sometimes it isn't the price that comes out on top. If there are offers that are similar but one has fewer conditions, the seller may choose the one with fewer conditions even if there is slightly less money on the table. Sometimes it comes down to a buyer being flexible about settlement.

These are high-pressure situations and they can be really stressful so you'll need to be clear in your mind from the outset what the property is worth to you and at what price you would think it best to walk away.

Even though agents work for the sellers, they have to take care to treat everyone involved in the sale fairly and ensure that the process is transparent. Their code of conduct requires that they do not put undue or unfair pressure on anyone to secure the sale.

If there were a very large number of offers made in a multi-offer scenario, the Real Estate Authority says it's possible to change this to a public auction, but in such cases everyone needs to be advised, and the auction conditions need to be prepared and presented to all parties.

## What's a mortgagee sale?

From time to time, you might see properties advertised as mortgagee sales. This is where the lender that provided a loan on a property is selling the property to repay the debt owed to the lender.

This is usually a last resort when people fall significantly behind on their loans.

While you can sometimes get a good price in a mortgagee sale, there are things to watch out for.

The first is that the person living in the property may not be happy about the sale. They might not make it easy for buyers to view the property and you have no guarantee that they won't do damage on the way out. There have been cases where people have taken pipes and even things like toilets with them. You can't count on chattels like curtains. There is no guarantee that the occupants will be out on the day that you take ownership.

The seller usually has the right to cancel the agreement any time until the deal settles, which can mean that you waste time and money on a deal that doesn't go through.

It may be a good idea to take out insurance on the property from the day you agree to buy the property.

## What's a set date sale?

You might sometimes see properties advertised with a 'set date of sale'. This is designed to build interest and create a sense of urgency to get buyers to act, and hopefully build some competition. It does not mean that you have until that date to think about whether you want to make an offer – offers can be accepted at any stage through the process.

## What's a tender?

A tender is a more formal process than a set date of sale, because the property will usually not sell before the tender date. If the vendor is keeping open the option of accepting an earlier offer, the advertising will say 'unless sold prior'.

In a tender situation, buyers give their offers, which are confidential, to the agent before a specified date. At that deadline, they are all opened together for the vendor to choose between.

If you are interested in a property going to tender, you should register your interest with the agent. This will mean you are informed if someone makes an early offer or the closing time changes.

Sometimes you'll get a price indication from a seller, but you can choose to offer whatever you like. You can put conditions on your offer, like needing to have finance approved or to conduct a property report. Sellers, in turn, can put their own conditions on the offer, such as specifying the date they want to sell.

Usually you'll be expected to offer a deposit with your tender offer. You'll need to talk to your lender about how you can make this happen.

## And what about an auction?

You probably have at least a vague idea of how a property auction works. Lots of people in a room, putting their hands up as a person talks really quickly, right?

Auctions are a popular method of sale for salespeople. They are good when it's not quite clear what a property is worth. That's the case when it's a place that's really unusual, or market conditions are changing (prices either rising or falling) and you can't be sure what buyers would be willing to pay.

For sellers, auctions are great when there is a lot of competition that pushes the price up beyond what those buyers would normally have offered. Sometimes the competitive spirit comes out in people and they keep bidding to win.

But auctions can be really bad for sellers when the market is soft. If you're in a room by yourself and realise you're the only person planning to bid, you might decide you're in a stronger negotiating position than you realised.

If you're keen on a property that is going to auction, the first thing to do is to register your interest and tell the salesperson you want to be kept up to date.

This means you'll know if the auction is being brought forward – this sometimes happens if an offer is made before the auction that the seller would accept. In this situation, they'd take that offer and make it the starting bid of the auction and hope someone else would bid it higher.

The salesperson will also send the legal documents through to your lawyer for them to review. This will include the deal you will sign if you are the successful bidder, setting out things like the settlement date. You can make changes to this agreement before the auction with something called a 'variation of agreement'. The seller will then decide whether they would accept those terms if you were the winning bidder.

Attend a few auctions where you don't plan to bid, so you can see what happens and be prepared.

The biggest difference between auctions and other methods of sale is that you need to have everything sorted before you bid.

You'll have to have completed all the building reports and valuations you need, as well as sorting your finances. That's because a bid is an unconditional offer. If you win, you have to go through with the purchase. Sometimes, when a property is going to auction, the vendor will have already prepared a

LIM or building inspection report, to help buyers get ready to bid on time.

You can ask your lawyer to help you work through the information you have about the property so you are prepared to bid. If you aren't getting a valuation, it's a good idea to use some of the property data sites to work out what the house might be worth. Check out whether any neighbours have sold recently and see how the place compares.

You'll usually pay your deposit on the day you win the auction. Make sure your finances are confirmed with your lender before you head into the auction room – the bank may want to know specific things about the house even if you have a preapproval to a certain amount.

When it comes time to bid, the auctioneer won't tell you what the reserve price is, but they will tell you when bidding reaches it.

Auctions are usually held either at the property that is for sale, in the real estate agency's rooms, or online.

You don't have to be physically in the room to bid on an auction. You can organise to bid via phone and it's becoming more common for auctions to be held virtually, too. Sometimes you may need to download an app to bid. You can also nominate someone to bid for you.

On the day of the auction, you may need to register when you arrive (or log in online). You will receive a bidder's number. Before bidding begins, the auctioneer will read the terms and conditions of the auction aloud, announce any important issues with the property, let bidders know whether the vendor is bidding and also disclose whether there are any registered online or phone bidders involved. Bidding will usually start below the reserve price.

A vendor bid will only be made before a property reaches a reserve, and is designed to keep the auction moving closer to the reserve price. It will be made clear to you when a bid is a 'vendor bid' so you understand whether you're competing with someone who really wants the property, or the existing owners.

As the auction goes along, the auctioneer will decide how much more each bid has to be than the one previous. Like other real estate salespeople, the auctioneer is trying to get the highest price possible for the property.

If bidding stalls before the auction reaches reserve, the salespeople involved might talk to the vendor about reducing their reserve in a effort to get things moving again. And if it doesn't reach reserve, the salespeople will usually negotiate with the top bidder to see if they can reach the price the vendor wants.

Sometimes there's a short period after the auction where the auction rules continue to apply – so if you make an offer within the next day and that offer is accepted, for example, you might find it has to be unconditional. But after this point, other buyers can put in their offers, too, including offers with conditions that meant they could not bid.

Successful bidders are asked to sign a sale and purchase agreement when the auction is over. If you're bidding online, the auctioneer might be able to do this for you.

## How much should you offer or bid?

It can be really hard to work out what the appropriate price is to pay for a property.

There are a few things I think are worth considering as you decide.

What are the neighbours selling for? Homes.co.nz and Trade Me Property are good places to look at what other properties nearby have sold for. If there are recent sales, you can often Google the address and see some photos of the property, to allow for a good comparison.

What is the current market like? If prices are rising quickly or you have a lot of competition, you might offer a higher price than you would if prices were softening and you were the only person interested.

What sort of seller are you dealing with? Understanding the motivations of the seller will help you to get a sense of what might be an appropriate offer. If someone is keen to get a deal done, whether that's a developer or an owner-occupier, they are usually more willing to consider lower offers. If they are just testing the market and in no hurry, you're probably wasting your time offering anything other than a really solid price.

General trends can help. Sometimes you can get data showing that a certain suburb is selling, on average, for a certain percentage above (or below) its CV. This can give you a sense of what might be appropriate for the region.

I think it's also really helpful to keep in mind that while it might not feel great to find out you've paid $20,000 more than you could have for a house, if you plan to live in it for a decade, it's likely that those small price differences will seem insignificant in time.

## What happens on settlement day?

The day you pay your money and the seller hands over the keys is called the settlement day.

Your bank sends the money to your lawyer, who passes it on to your vendor's lawyer, and the transfer of ownership is confirmed. Ideally, it all happens over one day, but it's likely that things may not go as smoothly or as quickly as you hope.

As a first-home buyer, you do have the advantage of not having to wait for another purchase to settle before the money can be transferred. But you still have to wait for the bank to send the money and, depending on how quickly the bank is moving and how many other transactions are being processed that day, it can take a while.

You will usually only get the keys, and access to the property, once the money has been paid into the vendor's solicitor's account.

You probably won't know this has happened until you get a call or email from your lawyer telling you that the sale has gone through and the change of ownership has been registered with LINZ.

The real estate agent may contact you to arrange picking up the keys. You'll also receive a copy of the new title with your name on it, and a statement from your lawyer showing what money was paid where, but this can sometimes take a day or two to come through.

If you're planning to move on settlement day, it's useful to have some flexibility in case things don't happen as fast as you like. It's frustrating to be paying for a moving truck that's stuck on the side of the road waiting for access to the new property.

If you agreed on vacant possession, as is the case for most first-home buyers, the sellers have to have completely left the property by the time you take ownership. If there is a delay at their end and that costs you money or time, such as paying extra for those movers, you can seek compensation from the sellers.

In a worst-case scenario, if something happens

that means the money can't be transferred on the settlement day, you will have to pay interest on the sale price until the deal can be done. The terms of this are included in your sale and purchase agreement.

## BUYER STORY:
### Phoenix

Phoenix says there was a bit of luck in how he and his wife, Jenn, came to find their house.

When they first started looking for properties, they were guided by what a mortgage broker told them they should be able to afford. At that stage, they could not get preapproval because they did not have a 20 per cent deposit.

'We went on a hunt for what we thought we would be able to get,' he says. 'We looked at eight to 10 houses every weekend and we would see the same people at all the houses. When we found a house we liked, we would typically put in an offer and someone would come in with a much higher offer and we would miss out.

'A lot of the time it would go to multi-offer and once your offer was in, it was in, and if you weren't the best you missed out. We had maybe three to six months of proactively booking in homes to see, going to open homes at the weekend.

'We had a friend who was renting a house and the landlord told them they were selling so we tried to negotiate with them but it ended up falling through.'

The couple moved in with Phoenix's parents during this time to save the money they would otherwise have spent on rent. They managed to save $90,000, including their KiwiSaver balances.

To get to the 20 per cent deposit that would allow them to get preapproval – and the ability to go to auctions – they needed another $30,000. Phoenix's parents offered to help by taking a loan and giving it to them. 'That was a big part of it.'

They found the house they eventually bought just before Christmas 2021.

'We came to look at the house and there weren't a lot of people here. Maybe people were waiting until the new year and it was a week or two before Christmas. There was only us and one other person considering putting an offer in. The real estate agent was quite helpful, she gave us a bit of inside information that other agents weren't giving us about the other offers. We went to up our offer and she told us not to because we were already the highest.'

The people selling did not yet have anywhere to move to, so the couple had to wait.

Phoenix now works two full-time jobs as well as a side hustle and contracting work to allow Jenn to stay home with the children and still pay the mortgage.

He says they felt lucky to have had support to get in the door.

'Without good support around you, it's quite difficult. What I've noticed is how lucky we were to have support, to move in with Mum and Dad and not pay. That's not something everyone has the ability to do. Without that, we wouldn't have been able to save the amount we saved. And without the contribution from Mum and Dad, we'd probably still be looking now.'

They looked at moving into a smaller rental while they searched for a house but realised the amount of rent that would save would be small compared to the inconvenience of squeezing the family into a smaller home.

'If you have support, that is key. Without that support, we would have found it hard.'

## BUYER STORY:
## Morgan

Morgan says she and her partner had become used to missing out on houses when they were hunting for theirs.

'We would go to open homes and two days later they would email us and say, "Sorry, the home has sold." Every single time. We would fall in love with a house, then ... it was so hard.'

The pair used their KiwiSaver money, sold a car and saved hard to pull together their deposit. They had both been in KiwiSaver since they started working as teenagers.

The first time they went to the bank to ask about a loan, they were told Morgan needed to earn more, so she changed to a different job that would give her more hours and a better pay rate.

'We had to get out of the house we were in at the time, so with the one we ended up getting we just put everything in. We needed a house. And our offer got accepted. We did what everyone else did to us, we went to the open home and then that night we made an offer.'

She said her partner's brother-in-law pointed out the house to them. At first, they thought it wouldn't be in their price range but when they visited the property, they discovered the advertisements might have overstated it. 'At first I said, "That is way out of our budget, it looks flash as . . ." but it wasn't that flash [in reality]. When we went to look we thought, "This isn't like the photos."'

There was a hold-up in the due-diligence phase when they were trying to confirm with the council that the fireplace had the required consents, but that was the only major hiccup, Morgan says.

'We've renovated the entire thing, which is amazing. It's nice having some kind of security, especially with how much rent is.'

She says it now probably costs them about as much to own as it would to rent. 'The mortgage is cheaper than our friends' rent, but with rates it's about the same.'

Morgan says the biggest piece of advice she would give other buyers is to have a budget and stick to it when you are saving your deposit. Once they decided they were really going to go for it, saving a deposit took three years.

'Write your budget down so you have something you can see.'

## Settlement checklist: Your countdown to moving day

☐ Pay the deposit once your offer is approved.

☐ Have your lawyer check the title of the property and confirm you are okay to proceed.

☐ Confirm that you have met all the requirements for finance from your lender and they are not waiting for any more information from you.

☐ Tick off all the requirements you listed as conditions of your purchase: property inspection report, LIM, valuation . . .

☐ Book a final pre-purchase inspection, where you check that everything is in working order and the things that you are expecting to be in place are still there. If anything is not working, or not as you expect, this is your chance to remedy it.

☐ Book a time with the lawyer ahead of settlement day to sign the mortgage documentation. If you are buying a unit title property, you will also need a copy of the body corporate's insurance policies, and the section 36 certificate (which refers to insurance), at least five working days before you settle.

☐ Book a moving company, if you're using one, and get packing boxes. More than you think you need.

## Refining your open-home strategy, and making an offer

☐ Separate out the things that you will want handy on moving day, such as a clean change of clothes, a jug and mugs for coffee, a set of cutlery, and set them aside so they don't get packed with the rest of your belongings.

☐ Arrange for someone to look after your kids and pets for moving day, if you can.

☐ Organise the utilities — set up a broadband and power account, etc.

☐ Redirect your mail (you can do this through the post office for up to a year at a time).

☐ Get house insurance in place for your new home.

☐ If your things aren't going from one place to another in one day, check what insurance you need for overnight storage.

# Chapter Nine

# LIFE WITH A MORTGAGE, AND OTHER COSTS

So you've got your mortgage, found your house and moved in. Congratulations! Getting in the door of your first home is a big achievement so it's worth taking some time to enjoy it (provided you know which packing boxes your champagne glasses are in to celebrate).

But in lots of ways, now you're just at the start. You have years of homeownership ahead of you, when you will be responsible for the maintenance and upkeep of the property as well as keeping up with your home loan repayments.

Here are some things you'll need to know upfront as you settle into your new life as a homeowner.

## Your mortgage

For lots of people, a major goal is to get rid of their loan as quickly as possible, although this can feel like a distant dream at the start when you are looking at a loan balance with lots of zeroes attached.

It's tempting to choose a mortgage rate, fix your loan and forget about it, but if you can be reasonably active in the management of your home loan you might be able to get rid of it more quickly.

Your first mortgage payment is probably going to be a small one as you get into the rhythm of principal and interest payments. You'll normally pay the amount you agreed to in repayments from the second instalment.

## Fixed or floating?

As part of the purchase process, your mortgage broker or bank will have wanted to know whether you want to fix your home loan.

Fixing means you lock your loan in at a specified interest rate for a fixed period of time. (If you still have bank branches in your neighbourhood, this means paying attention to some of those signs you see in the windows.) Advertised rates are a good guide to what is on offer, but you can often negotiate.

Locking in an interest rate is particularly helpful

in a period when rates are rising, or when you need certainty about what your payments will be.

Over the past 20 years, floating rates have – but not always – been more expensive than fixing.

New Zealanders tend to like fixing their loans more than people in other countries, even though we don't have the long-term options, like 20 or 30 years, that you see in the United States. (Though it should be noted that in the US it's different because 'fixed' borrowers can still reset their home loan interest rate lower.)

There have been attempts to introduce longer-term rates here, like seven or 10 years, but the take-up has been relatively low. People are reluctant to lock in rates for a long time, not knowing whether there would be better deals ahead. (And in retrospect, some of the longer-term loans advertised in 2015 preceded a very low-interest rate period where you might have been cursing your luck if you had taken one.)

When you fix your mortgage you are guaranteed to have paid a certain amount off at the end of the fixed term, but if you want to repay any extra you may have limited options.

## What's the right term to fix for?

Choosing the term for a fixed loan depends on your personal circumstances. You can usually fix for anything from six months to five years. If you have just moved into your house and you are still getting yourself sorted, working out what the bills will look like, you might be tempted by a longer fix. This will give you predictable repayments for longer and help you to wrangle your new budget, and maybe spend on some new homeowner costs like furniture, renovations or gardening work.

But you might find that after a year or so, you are in the groove and ready to step up your repayments, or you want to look for a better deal on your rate. It can be a good idea to keep an eye on the websites that display all the banks' interest rates so you can get an idea of what is on offer. Generally, one and two years are the most popular terms for owner-occupiers.

Picking the 'best' interest rate is a tough gig because it requires a bit of fortune-telling.

Over your lifetime, it is likely that you will go through periods when interest rates are higher and times when they are low. There's no guarantee about what is around the corner. A few people seemed to be caught by surprise when interest rates started to rise through 2022.

Nothing is constant in the interest-rate market – sometimes rates will seem to be rising, and sometimes they will look like they are falling. At some points in the interest rate cycle, the cheapest long-term strategy is a series of short-term fixes, like one or two years. But sometimes, a long-term rate actually proves to be a better option.

The problem is that, unless your crystal ball is functioning really well, it's hard to know what will prove to be the right call.

Long-term rates will usually have some of the predictions for the official cash rate and international funding costs priced in – so if these come in lower than predicted you could end up overpaying. But sometimes they haven't priced in a change that takes markets by surprise and a long-term fix turns out to be a good bet. Tricky, right?

You can look at forecasts from economists, like the ones the banks employ, to see where interest rates might be going but you'll need to bear in mind that they aren't always right. (In fact, they often get it quite wrong.) While it's usually semi-possible to pick where interest rates are going in the next year, unexpected things can pop up – hello, Covid – that change the picture. And the way the economy responds to events can be different to what economists expect – hello, Covid, again.

You'll probably cause yourself a lot of stress if you spend too much time trying to time the interest rate market to get the best possible deal.

A better strategy is to find a rate and term that feels comfortable for you every time you get a chance to refix. You might not get the cheapest rate in the market but if you get one that you can afford, and that enables you to keep paying down your loan in a way that fits your budget and circumstances, you can take that as a win.

Many people value certainty and are happy to spend a little more if it means they don't have to stress about rates rising for a while.

There might be some clear trends from time to time but generally it makes sense to use the rate that seems reasonable compared to what else is in the market, doesn't keep you up at night, but also gives you some flexibility if you need it.

If rates drop, it's a great opportunity to keep your repayments at the same level (which you know you can afford because you've already been paying this level) and pay off the loan faster. Some people say it isn't the rate of interest you pay but the rate at which you pay off your loan that matters – this can be a good rule to keep in mind if you are vexed about which term to choose.

If you decide you don't want the fixed term you signed up for any more – maybe because you've spotted a better rate that you wish you had taken or you are selling your house and getting out of the market – you will usually need to pay a break fee.

## What's a break fee?

A break fee is what you pay to cover the bank's costs when you break a fixed-term rate. When a bank offers you a fixed-term rate, it's usually based on the cost to the bank of borrowing the money it lends to you, plus a margin. If you decide you don't want to pay that fixed rate any more, it's likely the bank still has to keep paying whoever lent the money to it initially. That's usually a mix of local and offshore funding sources.

If rates have gone up since you fixed and the bank can easily find someone else to borrow the money and to pay the same or a higher rate than you were on, it probably won't bother to charge you a fee. It can just lend the money to someone else and get the same income. But if rates have gone down, it will have to lend that money to a new borrower for a lower rate – and it will look to cover the difference from you in a break fee. The calculations can be a bit confusing but the fee is generally representative of the amount of interest you have left to pay that is above what another, new borrower would pay in today's market.

If you sell a house with a fixed term in place you can often arrange with the bank to substitute the security and move the loan to a new property, so you do not have to break the loan and pay a fee.

Sometimes, if another lender is keen to pick up your business, it will offer to pay the break fee of your current bank to shift you over.

## Should you float for a bit?

You might wonder why people would have their loan floating at all if it's usually more expensive.

The biggest benefit to keeping your mortgage (or part of it) floating is that you are not locked in, in any way. If you want to pay off a chunk of what you owe, there is no penalty for that. You can also sell and close off the mortgage early without any extra cost.

And if rates start to move in a way that you are not comfortable with, you can choose to fix at any time. You pay a premium, but for some people that flexibility is really important. It can be especially handy if you are the type of person who earns money in an uneven way, because you can make big payments in the months when money is coming in and smaller ones in leaner periods.

## Revolving credit

You might have heard people talk about having a revolving credit home loan.

Revolving credit is basically like a huge overdraft, and offers some of the flexibility of a floating loan, as well as potentially mixing in some of the benefit of fixing.

Generally, you'll split off a portion of your loan and leave it floating while you fix the rest.

Then you have your pay directed into the floating part, so that each month your money is sitting there offsetting interest being charged. You put all your bills and other expenses on your credit card and then at the end of the month clear the card from the revolving credit account, hopefully leaving a bit of money in there to gradually pay off the amount owing over time.

You can then change another bit of your fixed loan to floating and repeat the process. Done well, this can help you get rid of a home loan much more quickly, but you do need some discipline.

You might see some home loan providers market revolving credit as a special feature but you can do it with any lender. As long as you have the self-control to stick to the plan and don't end up spending from both your revolving credit account and your credit cards, it can be a good option.

## Split it up

You don't have to just have one home loan.

In the same way you might carve off a bit to float as a revolving credit facility, you can divide up your loan into smaller bits and fix each for a different period.

This spreads your interest rate risk. When everything is fixed for five years, it means that in five years' time you are completely exposed to whatever interest rates are doing at that point. But if you fix a bit for one year, a bit for two and a bit for five, you'll only ever have some of your loan rolling off to refix.

Sometimes you might get a bargain and sometimes you might not, but you'll be able to spread your loan terms and get better rates when they become available, spreading your risk.

You can also choose to bump up your repayments, if you can. As each loan comes up for refixing, you get a chance to see if you could afford to repay a bit more. You might have had a pay rise that allows you to pay it off faster.

This is a good way to get some flexibility as well as certainty.

## What's the OCR and how does it affect the interest rate you pay?

*The official cash rate (OCR) is administered by the Reserve Bank.*

*It's a tool that's used to moderate activity in the economy. If the Reserve Bank is worried that inflation is rising too quickly, it can increase the OCR, which reduces the amount of disposable income many people and businesses have to spend. This should, in theory, reduce pressure in the economy and bring inflation back down.*

*If economic activity is weak and the bank wants to encourage more spending, it can reduce the OCR to give people more money to play with.*

*The rate is what banks pay for short-term lending from the Reserve Bank. It sets a base for what they then pay savers and charge borrowers – with a margin in there for their profit. It isn't the only driver of retail interest rates because banks can source money from other places, including offshore, but it tends to have quite a big impact on shorter-term home loan rates in particular.*

## Paying off your loan more quickly

It makes sense to want to get rid of your home loan as soon as you can. The longer you hold the loan, the more interest you pay.

You can pay off your loan faster by increasing your regular payments, making voluntary extra payments or paying off chunks in lump sums.

Banks will often let you increase your regular repayments by up to a specified amount without incurring any extra fees. The rules on this vary a bit so you'll need to check with your lender to see what it will let you do.

Usually you can increase payments within certain parameters, as long as you don't pay off more than a certain percentage in a year. Increasing your mortgage payments even a bit can save you a lot of money over your loan term. MoneyHub NZ calculates that if you have a $500,000 loan with a rate of 5 per cent with 30 years remaining, paying an extra $100 a month will save you $42,597 in interest and clear your loan three years faster.

You can also usually make a lump-sum payment on a fixed-term mortgage up to a certain amount without penalty. If you have a $500,000 loan fixed at 5 per cent with 30 years remaining, paying a ump sum of $30,000 would save you more than $90,000 in interest. When interest rates are higher, you can potentially save more.

If you have part of your mortgage floating, there is no penalty for any extra amount you want to repay on that part.

You can also pay off your loan more quickly by switching from monthly payments to fortnightly. Sound weird? It works if you take the monthly amount and divide it in two. This effectively gives you an extra monthly payment a year, because there are 26 fortnights a year. For a $500,000 loan on

4 per cent interest, that could save you almost $60,000 in interest over the full mortgage term.

## Maintenance

Being stuck with a home maintenance bill is one of the few downsides for people who shift from renting to homeownership.

You won't have a landlord to ring when something goes wrong, so it's helpful to have some money available in case of urgent repairs.

Hopefully you'll have had a building report done when you were considering buying the house, which will have highlighted any major work on the horizon.

If you discover a serious issue that you think you should have been told about by the real estate salesperson, the Real Estate Authority advises that you should gather all your relevant documentation, such as the building report, LIM and the sale and purchase agreement you signed.

Dig out any correspondence you had with the agent or private seller, or make notes of the conversations that you remember. Add any information you have about the property now, then think about what outcome you want. Are you after compensation or do you just want someone to sort out the problem?

Your lawyer is a good first stop for any issue like this — they can help you negotiate with the seller or salesperson or help you take action. You'll be in the strongest position if you can prove that they knew about a problem and deliberately didn't tell you.

If it turns out that the real estate agent acted poorly, and won't help you resolve the problem, you can complain to the Real Estate Authority.

Beyond that, the Building Research Association (BRANZ) estimates it costs about 0.5 per cent to 2 per cent of the value of a house annually, excluding the land, to keep it in good condition. This is hardly ever distributed smoothly – one year you might have no repairs or maintenance and the next you might have a big bill.

New houses might have no issues at the start but a rush of them a bit further down the track. That figure is a reasonable guide to what you should expect to have to prepare for, though.

You'll have a sense of what repairs and improvements are the most important, but it's usually a good idea to do things like wiring and electrics as a priority, and fixing leaks.

If you're doing up the house, projects that typically improve the value include kitchen and bathroom renovations (provided you don't spend so much money that you can't recover it if you want to sell), insulation, landscaping that makes the garden more usable for entertaining and new garage doors.

That last one might seem weird but I've seen a

lot of examples of houses with internal garages that suddenly look much newer with a brand new, insulated door.

Things like pools and built-in sound systems are less likely to add value. Pools aren't always seen as a positive by buyers (some mad people think of them as a major hassle to look after) and built-in electrics can date really fast.

## Rates

You'll also have to pay rates, usually to your local council and regional council and there are sometimes separate water rates, depending on where you are in the country.

These are usually billed quarterly, but you can set up a direct debit to pay more frequently if that suits you better.

When you bought the house, the vendor would have paid rates up to the date the property changed hands. Usually what happens is the vendor pays the next chunk of rates to the council, and then the amount that relates to the time from when you'll be in the house is paid by you when you buy the house.

For example, if your vendor had a rates bill that covered September to December, and you bought in November, the vendor would probably have already paid the rates to December, and you'll reimburse them for the November and December portion as part of your purchase transaction.

Rates cover things that the council pays for. Your rates bill will go towards new public developments, the maintenance of public facilities, some roads, libraries, swimming pools and so on. Be warned, rates do tend to rise.

## CV (capital value)

You probably became fairly well acquainted with property CVs when you were hunting for a house.

These are the values that are assigned to all the homes in the city every three years by a property valuation firm working for the council.

They determine how the rates cost is spread among all the homeowners in the council area. Generally, more valuable properties have bigger rates bills but there is quite a lot of variation around the country.

Having your CV increase won't, by itself, mean you face a bigger rates bill.

But if you own a property that increases in value faster than others, you could end up having a bigger increase. Generally, your property's CV will mean very little to you during the time you own the house. It's only a representation of what it would have sold for at a particular point in time, and it's done as a desktop exercise without visiting, so it's quite a blunt tool.

You'll know from your buying experience that what people are willing to pay can vary wildly.

If you are ever worried that your CV is too low (probably only if you are trying to get buyers to pay top dollar) or too high (if you think it's out of whack with your neighbours and you're paying more rates as a result) you can ask for it to be reassessed.

## Insurance

You will need to budget for insurance. It's likely that building insurance was a requirement for you getting a home loan in the first place – banks like to make sure that the properties they are holding as security will still exist even if there is a fire or natural disaster. But you'll also need contents insurance and to make sure that your policies are kept valid, and with the correct sum insured (if that's the type of policy you have).

You may also want to take out life insurance so that your partner isn't left with a loan to pay by themselves if something were to happen to you. Depending on your circumstances, income protection insurance could also be useful. Weigh up your options and consider what risks you might be exposed to and which you are happy to live with.

## What if the market softens?

You've probably heard people say things like 'house prices double every 10 years', or 'house prices only ever go up'.

While that might be true over the long term, they don't always go one way when we are talking about shorter chunks of time.

Prices can move down as well as up, as we saw in 2022. This can be pretty disconcerting, especially if you've battled for years to get the money together for a purchase, only to see the value of that house seemingly slip.

But as long as you can hang on, owning is usually a better bet in the long run.

It's the sticking with it that is key. Data shows that when people sell, it's almost always those who have had a short 'hold time' that incur the biggest losses.

In the first quarter of 2022, about 1 per cent of sales were for less than their owners had bought them for. The median amount of loss was $37,500. In the second quarter it was 2 per cent and the median loss was $40,000. Back in 2010 and 2011, the proportion of loss-making sales was much higher – about 20 per cent. In an earlier downturn, in 2002, more than 25 per cent of sales were for a loss.

When prices are softening, it can be hard to imagine that things will ever turn around.

You'll probably have visions of being stuck in your house in negative equity for years. But try to keep your eyes on the long term – you're paying off your loan, you're already in a house you (hopefully) like. As long as you don't have to move, any loss in value is only on paper.

These days, you're unlikely to end up in negative equity (when you owe more than the property you have borrowed against is worth) because in recent years banks have required borrowers to have significant deposits. Very few people are taking out loans over 90 per cent any more, which means even a major drop would not put many borrowers underwater.

The bank will also have checked that you can meet your repayments. Sometimes, in a weaker market, you can improve your property to boost its value but you need to be careful not to overcapitalise (spend more than you can recoup) in this scenario.

Median price movements can also be deceptive – while your suburb might drop in value, it's possible that you bought well, or your house is particularly awesome (of course) and so your value might not move as much as some.

In the worst-case scenario, provided you have enough equity to do so, if you were to move on from your house to another, it would potentially be similarly valued at a lower amount, so you don't really lose out. And if everything drops 10 per cent, entry-level houses lose less value in dollar terms than the place you might move to as a next step.

If you keep your head down, and focus on why you bought a house in the first place – maybe to provide stability or give you more control over your life – you will probably find that in a few years' time you will look back and realise that you are in a much better position than you would be if you had not bought.

And while you might see stories of people nabbing a bargain and feel that FOMO, it's worth remembering that lots of people don't list their properties when the market is weak, so you might not have been able to find a house you liked as much, even if you had held on for a softer market.

As with any sort of investing, accept that being in a market comes with some ups and downs. Focus on the things you can control, like paying off your home loan.

## And what if, after all that, you decide homeownership isn't for you?

You might decide, after going through this exercise, that owning a home isn't something that you aspire to after all, or at least, not right now.

That's totally fine. In lots of countries around the world, it's not unusual for people to rent for most, if not all, of their lives.

More attention is now being paid to renters' rights and it may be that renting in the future is a much more secure and comfortable prospect than many people find it to be at present.

You can usually afford to rent a more expensive property than your budget would allow you to buy, and if you value freedom and flexibility, renting can be a good option.

That's particularly true if you are able to save the difference between rent and the cost of owning a house, and invest it somewhere that will give you a good return.

Being a renter can sometimes be a problem when you get to retirement, so you might need to do some extra planning. Homeowners might hope to be debt-free by the time they stop working, and a mortgage can be a pricey sort of enforced savings.

But renters won't ever have their rent bills stop unless they can find a way to move in with family or friends or another rent-free accommodation option. (Although it should be noted that if you are a renter in retirement, you won't have lots of other costs that come with owning a home, like rates, maintenance and insurance.)

This means that if you are planning to rent long-term, you'll need to save a bit extra to cover the costs you encounter when you finish work. It's possible that you may be able to qualify for some government assistance but that depends on the rules and criteria that apply at the time you retire.

Another option could be to aim to save enough to buy a house in a cheaper area that you don't plan to live in while you are working but could be a comfortable option when you retire.

It is worth getting some personalised financial advice if you are taking the non-buying route, to make sure you are on track. There are other investments that you can pursue, like the sharemarket, that should help your money keep pace with inflation more effectively than it would in a bank account.

## BUYER STORY:
## Davinia

Davinia says it was a long process to get into her first home with her partner, Jade, and their children. At first, it seemed more like a dream than something they could actually imagine happening, she says.

When they first moved into Kaikohe, they would look at houses for sale and daydream about what it might be like to buy them.

'I thought I was never going to buy a house,' Jade says. 'Davinia said we should try to buy and

I said, "No, we wouldn't ever be able to afford it." I wanted to, but I just never thought about it because it seemed so difficult.'

But they wanted a home for their four children to grow up in and the idea stayed in the back of their minds.

The first time they applied for a loan, they were turned down. 'There was too much Afterpay, paying off stuff, bills. They said, "Get rid of all this and then apply again in six months,"' Davinia says.

They spent the time tidying up their finances, and sold a truck, which helped to bolster their deposit.

'We had a four-wheel drive and one of the reasons we sold it was that it wasn't going to suit our family when I got pregnant again,' Davinia says. 'We're a family of six now and it was a five-seater so it wasn't going to suit the family but we sold it and paid off a lot of bills with that money and put some in savings as well, which really helped.'

The pair had money in KiwiSaver and worked to save a 10 per cent deposit across that and a savings account.

They kept their spending as low as possible by living in a cheap rental.

'We were living in a two-bedroom unit with five of us at the time. It was really small but it was cheap and it was the only way we were going to save money. 'We had to stick it out for two years. It was getting too small for us and we were tempted to move into a three- or four-bedroom rental so we would have space but then we were going to have to spend more money on renting a house when the plan was to save money for a house we could pay off for ourselves. We saved quite a bit of money that way as well.'

The house they ended up buying seemed out of their price range at first.

'We thought we would go and have a look and thought it was cool but we couldn't afford it. We applied with the best offer we could afford but it was a multi-offer with three other people and we weren't successful at that point.'

But the house stayed listed for sale on Trade Me and about a month later, the salesperson got back in touch to say it hadn't sold, and to ask whether the couple was still interested.

'We tried to play it off, like, "Oh we could be, but we're looking at a couple of other properties,"' Jade says.

'There was a bit of back and forth between us and the agent and we said we'll probably offer a little bit more than we offered before. We were still far below the asking price but they accepted it.'

The final offer was $28,000 less than the house had been advertised for. The couple said the broker they worked with was helpful when it came to working through the purchase process.

'We had no idea what we were doing. As we were doing things and sending things through, the broker was saying you need to do this and do that, you need to get a lawyer. We thought, "We need to get a lawyer?" We did a lot of it blindly, really, and then the lawyer came into place and the broker had to explain all the things we had to do, getting the building report, the LIM report … we didn't realise there is a lot of money to be spent before purchasing a house.'

Prices were rising fast at the time and the pair were glad they got in when they could to secure a home for their kids.

A different house they daydreamed about when they started looking is now just down the road. 'Even now when we walk past we think "it's such a cool house" but prices have gone up so quickly since we moved up. Maybe $100,000 or more in the last two years,' Davinia says.

Chapter Ten

# ARE YOU READY TO BECOME AN INVESTOR?

Once you're in the door of your first house, you might start thinking about investing in other properties.

It's quite likely that, through the buying process, you encountered enough landlords to understand a bit about how they work. Maybe you caught the property bug and can't switch off your desire to appraise what a place might be worth when you drive by.

You wouldn't be alone. Property investment is one of the major ways that New Zealanders have built their wealth over the years. And many people have done extremely well out of it. The value of New Zealand's housing stock had hit $1.7 trillion at the start of 2022.

There are lots of reasons why people like investing in property. It's something you can see and touch. While you might put money into shares, that can seem like quite an abstract concept. When you own an investment property, you can go and visit it, if you want to (and provided you give the tenant enough notice).

We also tend to have a better understanding of how property investment works than many other asset classes, because housing is such a big part of people's financial lives.

Until recently, there were other tax breaks that made it an appealing investment, too. For a while, you could claim the home loan interest you paid on an investment property against the income you earned from your day job, reducing your tax bill. That was then pulled back so the losses could only apply to the income from the property itself, before Labour moved to phase out the deduction option completely, except for new builds. (Though it should be noted, as mentioned earlier, that National has indicated it would undo this.)

Capital gains have also been delivered largely tax-free. Those gains have been big – homes.co.nz estimated that even in mid-2022, when prices had been falling pretty steadily for six months, most cities still had values that were at least twice the level they had been eight years earlier.

The introduction of the brightline test has changed

that a bit, but provided you hold a property for long enough, and didn't buy it with the intention of selling to make a profit, you can still bank a tax-free gain.

Investing in property can be a good way to build your wealth. But things have become a bit more complicated in recent years, so it's extra important to know what you are doing before you jump in.

## What's your strategy?

One of the first things you'll need to work out is why you are investing. Are you looking for rental income, to provide a (semi) passive flow of money into your bank account? Or are you looking for a property that will increase in price and give you a big return when you sell? Or maybe you're looking for properties that you can do up and flip?

Knowing what you want to achieve from the outset is important because it will guide your purchasing decision.

Sharon Cullwick, a property expert who recently headed up the New Zealand Property Investors Federation, is in favour of focusing on yield. That is the calculation of the amount of rent that a property pulls in compared to the purchase price. If you buy a property for $600,000 and let it for $500 a week, that gives you a rental yield of 4.17 per cent. That's not the net yield because from that you have to cover the costs of owning the property, but it gives you a way to compare investments.

You'll also have to cover things like maintenance, rates, administration costs and any vacancies between tenants.

Cullwick says it's important to focus on yield because a property should be able to pay for itself. 'At the moment they are few and far between but you need to get as close as possible, in case something happens, you lose your job and can't afford to keep putting money into the investment.'

A property that delivers good amounts of rent compared to the purchase price will be easier to hold on to, which means you aren't forced to sell in a downturn, when you might not get a good price for the property.

She says that while people often do make big capital gains out of their investments, that should not be the focus. Capital gains should be a bonus that you're not counting on.

Cullwick says a lot of investors have a benchmark of looking for a property that will deliver a yield at least two percentage points higher than interest rates. If you are going to be paying 4 per cent for your home loan, you want the property to be returning at least 6 per cent of its purchase price in rent each year.

Another investor, Graeme Fowler, who features in the media regularly as the investor who owns 70 or

80 properties, says he would be looking for at least 6 per cent at the moment.

Cullwick says you can maximise your yield by looking at properties with dual incomes, such as a house with a granny flat that can be rented out separately.

## Capital gains

Following a capital gains strategy is a bit riskier because you're at the mercy of the market to a larger degree. But it does seem to be a common strategy – data shows that many investors are barely breaking even.

In this case, you'd probably be buying properties in areas that had strong growth potential rather than high rents compared to the purchase price. Generally, more expensive places to buy do not have comparably higher rents, so the yields are lower.

But if, for example, prices increased by 15 per cent across a city, the properties that started at $2 million would experience a bigger increase in dollar terms than those that started at $700,000.

Capital gains–driven investors also look for areas where there is potential for development, and where they may become sought after by buyers in future. This is back to the same sort of idea I discussed earlier – looking for areas where infrastructure is being built and new amenities are becoming available.

Some people are happy to carry negatively geared properties (these are properties that do not pay for themselves, and require the owner to top up the mortgage payments out of their own money) if they can see capital gains down the track.

But these look like less of a good investment when the market is soft.

A capital-gains strategy is a winner when the market is on your side, but there is no guarantee. For now, it seems that prices are cooler and it's unlikely that we're going to see the 30 per cent-plus increases in a year again for a while. The huge price increases we saw during 2020 and 2021 were driven by a pretty unusual set of factors – super-low interest rates collided with incomes holding up better than expected and people being unable to spend their money overseas as they normally would.

If you're in it for capital gains, you'll need to be prepared to stick with it for quite a while, and know you can make it through various economic conditions.

## Doing up and flipping

If you are good at DIY and have a good idea of what the market wants, you can make good money from doing up properties and selling them. That's particularly true when the market is buoyant.

Provided you can stick to a budget and do not

overcapitalise, sometimes small cosmetic changes can make a significant difference.

But you may find that these transactions are caught by the brightline test, and you end up paying tax on them. That's the case if you already own a home and are doing this on secondary properties, or if you do a lot of flips in a short period of time.

At the other end of the spectrum, if the work you do is so significant that you end up with a new Code Compliance Certificate issued, you may be able to claim the property as a new build and get the tax benefits that go with that.

Some people opt to do up and revalue a house to boost the equity on their balance sheet. That can sometimes give them enough of a deposit to borrow again and purchase another investment property.

## Getting finance for an investment

As I mentioned earlier, it can be a bit harder to get a loan for an investment property than for an owner-occupied home.

Banks tend to be tougher with applications from investors than from first-home buyers. Depending on the loan-to-value restrictions at the time, you'll have to have a bigger deposit and you'll need to prove that you have the income to service the loan.

At the time of writing, the requirement for

investors was a deposit or equity in the deal of at least 40 per cent, except if they were buying a new-build property.

Lenders usually only take anything from 65 per cent to 75 per cent of predicted rental income into consideration when deciding whether you can afford to repay a property investment loan. This allows for periods of vacancy, as well as any extra costs that could come your way.

If you're starting to invest, you might have a deposit already saved. But you might want to borrow against the equity in your home, which is a really common way of becoming an investor.

It works like this.

Say you bought your house for $800,000, with a mortgage of $600,000. At this point your LVR is 75 per cent, which is enough to keep the banks happy as an owner-occupier, but not enough to spread to any investment properties.

But after a few years, your property has increased in value to $1.2 million. You've probably also paid off a bit of your mortgage in that time.

At this point, you can redraw against your house's new value, probably to a maximum of 80 per cent LVR, depending on the loan-to-value restriction settings at the time.

That means you can take your mortgage back out to $960,000 or thereabouts, giving you another

$360,000 to put into another property. Depending on the LVR rules, that may need to constitute 40 per cent of the purchase price, which means you can buy a new investment property for up to $900,000.

This means you effectively increase your borrowing by the full purchase amount, albeit secured across two properties, so the bank will also test to make sure that with your existing income and the rental income you'll get for the investment property, you'll be able to service the loans.

This obviously works really well in situations where prices are rising fast and people are building equity quickly in their properties. It's not such a great solution when prices are flat, although you can still build equity by doing up your property and having it revalued, or paying down your home loan more quickly.

## *Benefits of a new build*

*New-build properties have a few benefits as an investment. They are exempt from the loan-to-value restrictions, so you may find it easier to get a loan. You can also claim home loan interest on a new build against rent income, for tax purposes, for 20 years. New builds are also only captured by the brightline test, which requires gains to be taxed at an investor's marginal tax rate, for five years, rather than 10.*

## Finding the right property

The next question is what to invest in.

When you're buying a home to live in, you can get a bit emotional about the process and fall in love with a cute fireplace or gorgeous garden for the kids to play in. When you're investing, you need to be a bit more hard-nosed.

Who will rent the property? How much will they pay? How much it will cost you for the upkeep? It's also vital to make sure that the property meets the current requirements for a rental – or won't be too expensive to bring it up to the standards. That ancient fireplace that you might have thought was charming for your own place could end up being a major Healthy Homes problem. You will need to make sure that any property you are looking at meets the government's Healthy Homes standards (See pages 279–281). Even something as simple as incorrect drainage can create a pricey problem. You can have a property assessed for this before you purchase.

Fowler says that when he got started, it was a case of trial and error. He's told media how he lost $40,000 on his first property, seven years after he bought it in 1994. 'It took 18 months to save my first deposit from age 22 to 24 and I saved $25,000 starting from nothing,' he told me in 2019.

'The property I bought in Wellington turned out to be a terrible decision and I ended selling it seven years later for a $40,000 loss. But it was the best thing that could have happened, because I learned so much from that, so many lessons.'

If you want to avoid having to learn these lessons yourself, he says there are a few things to think about.

You might look at an apartment in a bigger city. These have the advantage of coming with a relatively low price, but also have more ongoing costs from the body corp, maintenance of the building and management fees. You'll need to stay well clear of anything that might have remedial issues.

He says that in smaller cities, you could look at two- or three-bedroom units or stand-alone houses.

'While I've had many of each – units, flats and houses – I prefer stand-alone houses, but it's only my preference,' he says.

A stand-alone property might give you more maintenance to deal with than a unit but you will also have more say about what happens with the property and will not be dictated to by a neighbour.

Some investors choose to invest in an area close to them so that they can keep an eye on the property and manage it themselves. Others opt for somewhere cheaper in the country.

It is important to understand the dynamics of the area you are investing in.

What looks like a bargain to someone in Auckland might not seem like such a great deal to someone who lives locally and hasn't yet become numb to $1 million houses.

House prices on the West Coast, for example, can look extremely cheap to someone coming into the area. But that doesn't mean that you'll necessarily make a big gain from buying one. In January 2022, a Buller house sold for $55,000 less than it cost to buy 12 years ago. You would need to make sure the rental income was sufficient to make holding a property like that worthwhile.

If you're considering an area other than your own to buy in, think about things like where people will work. If there is strong employment, that means more people may move into the area, and if they are being paid well they may be able to afford higher rents.

What sort of tenants will you attract, and how does the property suit them? Some areas are full of young families and you won't find as much demand for small units. But in others, there's a big student population or older people who live alone and don't mind a one- or two-bedroom place.

Look at what other properties are around, too. If there is a shortage of rental properties it will be easier for you to find tenants than if yours is one of hundreds listed for rent. How is the local economy holding up? This might give you a guide to where the future direction of rent might go.

## Managed apartments

*Some of the cheapest investment properties you'll spot on your search might be managed apartments.*

*These are usually in a hotel complex, and are let out to guests staying there.*

*There can be benefits – you don't have to worry about management of the property, and your place will be regularly cleaned and checked on.*

*But the property will often have higher rates if it's a commercial operation, and you might not get the rent yield you expect.*

*You are usually limited in how much you can access the property (if at all) and you'll need to understand what you are committing to in the lease. It can be very hard to remove the property from the pool of managed apartments, should you want to.*

You can also consider the property price cycles and where each region might be in those. While we talk about overall median prices for the country, each region tends to move at a slightly different pace. If you notice that prices have picked up in other parts of the country but not yet in the area you are looking at, you may be able to get a good buy.

You'll usually have the most demand from tenants if you have a property that is near good public transport links, shops and schools. Fowler recommends focusing on somewhere that has a population of at least 50,000.

Cullwick cautions that if you're not buying somewhere close to you, you will also need to budget for a property manager to keep an eye on it. This can cost about 8 to 8.5 per cent of your rental income.

She says investors should not be afraid of looking at lower socioeconomic areas. 'Often the rents are subsidised, paid by the government.'

Generally, the best rental properties are relatively simple, with as small a number of things that could go wrong and need attention as possible. Many people go for ex-state houses for this reason, because often – apart from needing a coat of paint every so often – they are solid and reliable.

Cullwick also cautions staying away from anything that could be deemed an illegal dwelling. Usually this will be somewhere that doesn't have the correct consent to be used as a residential property, such as a garage or commercial property that has been repurposed. There have been cases where tenants have been awarded their rent back when they have gone to the Tenancy Tribunal.

## Healthy Homes requirements

The standards that rental properties have to meet:

- Landlords must provide one or more fixed heaters that can directly heat the main living room. The heater(s) must be acceptable types, and must meet the minimum heating capacity required for your main living room.
- The World Health Organization (WHO) recommends a minimum indoor temperature of 18 °C. So, tenants will be able to keep warm all year round.
- Ceiling and underfloor insulation has been compulsory in all rental homes since 1 July 2019. The Healthy Homes insulation standard

builds on the current regulations and some existing insulation will need to be topped up or replaced. The level of insulation required depends on where in the country you are.

- In each room, the size of the openable windows, doors and skylights together must be at least 5 per cent of the floor area of that room.
- Each door, window or skylight must be openable and must be able to remain fixed in an open position.
- All kitchens and bathrooms must have either an extractor fan that vents air to the outside or a continuous mechanical ventilation that meets certain criteria.
- Rental properties must have efficient drainage for the removal of storm water, surface water and ground water. Rental properties with an enclosed sub-floor space must have a ground moisture barrier.
- Landlords must make sure the property doesn't have unreasonable gaps or holes in walls, ceilings, windows, skylights, floors and doors that cause noticeable draughts. All unused open fireplaces must be closed off or their chimneys must be blocked to prevent draughts.

Source: Tenancy Services NZ

## Accidental landlords

Sometimes, people become landlords when they decide to hold on to a property and rent it out when they move on, rather than selling it.

This can work if the property you currently live in is in a sought-after rental area.

But the sorts of houses we choose as owner-occupiers are often a bit different to the sort that work well as a rental property. There might be more upkeep involved, or gardens that have been built up and need looking after.

It's worth putting emotion to the side and deciding whether your house stacks up as a rental investment. If you were shopping for a rental property now, would you choose it?

It could be that you are better to sell the property while it's still in good condition and use the proceeds to invest in another place. While tenants can be great and treat a property well, they won't be as invested in the property and it may begin to show after a while.

## *Guaranteed rent?*

*You might see property managers offering 'guaranteed rent' if you place your property with them. There's usually a catch – if a property manager is offering to cover rent for any vacant weeks, they will usually charge you a higher fee.*

*You can, however, choose to lease a property to Kāinga Ora as social housing in return for guaranteed monthly payments.*

## Tax

You'll probably need to get an accountant on your side to help you navigate your leap into being a landlord.

There have been a lot of changes on the tax front for investors in recent years.

As noted earlier, the Labour government decided to phase out investors' ability to offset their home loan costs against their rental income to reduce their tax bills. This means that you pay tax on the entire rent you receive, minus expenses such as property management fees, rates and insurance – and then pay your home loan off separately.

The brightline test has also been extended. This is the test that determines whether you should pay tax on any profits you make from the sale of a property. At the moment, any existing house you buy as an investment will be subject to tax on the sale profits if you sell again within 10 years.

Because this tax is applied at the taxpayer's marginal tax rate in the year you sell, you could end up paying 39 per cent on most of the gains if your annual income plus the gains from the property add up to more than $180,000.

An accountant can advise you on the best structure to purchase a property. You might choose to own property in your own name, or through a partnership, trust or company.

## Managing tenants

When you own a property investment, you aren't just dealing in houses – you're providing a home for someone to live in.

Dealing with tenants can be one of the trickiest aspects of being a landlord.

You can choose to manage the property yourself, but it is a good idea to have a thorough understanding of your responsibilities and rights in relation to the property. There are restrictions on what can be agreed to in a tenancy agreement, and new guidelines on what can be asked at which point of a tenancy application. There are good online resources that can help with this.

You'll need to have a back-up person in place in case something goes wrong when you are on holiday.

If you decide to employ a property manager, you can delegate a lot of the work. They will do things like regular inspections of the property (these are usually required to keep your insurance current) and deal with queries from the tenants when something needs to be fixed. A good property manager will also make sure that you keep up with the changing rules and regulations of the rental market. But you will pay for the service.

Fowler says the cost of a property manager almost always pays for itself.

'I would also have the property managed by a good property manager, especially when you are starting out as a landlord. People often avoid this to save themselves money, but in almost all cases it ends up costing them a lot more than they thought they were going to save,' he says.

'I still think property, even with all its many changes, is a great way for people to build wealth over time if it's done correctly.

'There are many pitfalls that can catch people out so it's important to learn as much as you can before you buy your first property. This can be done by reading books on property investing, joining your local property investor association or joining one of the online property chat groups on Facebook. I set one up several years ago which now has 60,000 members and a wealth of information and many experienced investors who are part of it. In that way, there's a lot more readily accessible information available now than even 10 years ago.'

## Landlord responsibilities

When renting out a property, landlords need to:
- make sure the property is in a reasonable condition
- let the tenant have quiet enjoyment of the property
- meet all relevant building, health and safety standards
- handle any abandoned goods in the correct way
- inform the tenant if the property is for sale
- have an agent if they are out of New Zealand for more than 21 days.

Landlords can't:
- seize the tenant's goods for any reason
- interfere with the supply of any services to the premises, unless it is necessary to prevent danger to a person or to allow repairs.

Source: Tenancy Services NZ

# READY, SET, GO!

Wherever you are at on your path to homeownership, I hope this book has helped you work out how to get where you want to be as soon as you can.

Here's the TLDR version, for if you're in a hurry.

## Your 25-step plan to homeownership

1. Take 10 minutes and have a good look at your bank accounts. Are they in good shape? Are you going into overdraft when you shouldn't? Are your bills being paid on time? Are your credit cards being paid in full? Get your spending in order if it's not already.

2. Start saving. Whether that's putting money into your KiwiSaver (if you will qualify to be able to withdraw it) or in a separate savings vehicle, like

a bank account or a different sort of managed fund, is up to you. But start putting money aside regularly. Make sure you're putting at least enough into your KiwiSaver account to get the full government contribution and as much as you qualify to have matched by your employer.

3. Save as much as you can without taking all the fun out of your life. A short, sharp burst of savings might get you started but you'll need to find an equilibrium that you can live with for a while so you can build up a solid deposit.

4. Boost your income if you can. If you can't get a pay rise, consider a side hustle or contracting work that you can do outside your normal job to bring in some extra money.

5. Check whether there are any costs that you can trim from your budget. Are there any subscriptions being paid each month that you don't actually need, or memberships to the gym you're not using? Watch out for any annual subscriptions that you might have forgotten about.

6. In the months leading up to your application, try to keep your spending as 'clean' as you can. Banks are particularly worried about anything that looks like a habit or an ongoing commitment.

7. Close any credit cards you don't need – the bank will take the full limit into account, not just the

amount you are using when assessing how much debt you have.

8. Get in touch with a mortgage broker to talk about what you might qualify for. Don't wait until you think you're almost ready to buy – you can check in with a broker at any stage to get a guide on what you might eventually qualify for and what you need to do to get the best chance of success.

9. Start looking at houses for sale in your area and follow them through until the deal is done (you'll see the sale price listed on sites like homes.co.nz eventually, or the salesperson may tell you). This will give you a good idea of what places are actually selling for. Listed prices are not always a good guide.

10. Identify a lawyer you can work with when it's time to make an offer.

11. Scout out potential areas you might want to live in, so you understand the amenities. Talk to friends in the area so you know to watch out for any potential fishhooks.

12. Head to a couple of auctions so you get a feel for what they are like.

13. When it's time to start looking, cast your net as wide as you reasonably can. Think about 'hidden gem' suburbs that you might not know about but that might have homes that suit your needs. Ask around – your friends may know of people who

have recently bought first homes and can report on what those areas are like to live in. Media will sometimes run 'suburb report'-style pieces that could give you an insight into areas you might not have considered.

14. Don't be afraid to ask lots of questions when you get to open homes. The more information you have, the better.

15. Understand how much you can afford to offer and stick within a range that is comfortable for you, even if the bank says you could handle more. Although the banks are pretty good at checking serviceability (it's part of the rules they have to live by), only you know how you manage your money day to day and how much of a buffer you need to feel okay.

16. If you're in a multi-offer situation, put your best foot forward but don't let the salesperson put you under undue pressure. There will always be another house.

17. Don't put too many conditions on your offer but add everything you need. While you don't want to add so many conditions that it is unworkable (and in theory you could add basically any condition you like), you should feel entitled to add all the conditions that you think will make you feel good about your purchase, like getting a building report. Make sure you have allowed

adequate time to confirm finance, even if you are preapproved to a set amount.

18. If you are planning to bid at auction, make sure you have every box ticked before you turn up. If you are the successful bidder, it counts as an unconditional offer.

19. When your offer is successful, start setting up plans for your big move. You will probably need to organise power and broadband connections, and maybe a mail redirection. If you want to use movers, book them early. Put insurance in place for the house, and maybe for yourself, too.

20. Book a final pre-purchase inspection to check everything is as you expect it to be, and that the occupants haven't caused damage since you put your offer in, for example. This is a good time to get any minor problems remedied. Your building report should have picked up any major issues earlier.

21. Be prepared to wait for settlement on the big day. It can take more time than you expect for your money to make its way from your bank to the vendor's solicitor. The real estate agent will usually give you the keys once the transaction is complete.

22. Structure your mortgage in a way that suits your circumstances. Some people like the certainty of a long-term fix, while others are happy to ride the ups and downs in return for an overall smaller

interest bill (usually).

23. Dividing up your loan into smaller parts may give you more flexibility – you won't have your entire loan exposed to a refix at any one time.

24. Take the opportunity to pay off your loan as fast as you can. Even small payment increases can make a big difference over the term of your loan.

25. If prices drop, try not to worry about it. Property is a long-term thing and over the long run, you should be better off from being a homeowner.

Homeownership isn't something that suits everyone, but for the vast majority of New Zealanders it's a really important part of their wealth, and it can make a big difference to their quality of life.

Now that prices have calmed down a bit after their Covid Chaos (maybe I should trademark that?) we should hopefully see things settle and become slightly less daunting for first-home buyers.

## Tips from the experts

To set you off on the right track, I asked a number of financial experts what advice they would give to first-home buyers.

## Hannah McQueen, financial coach and founder of enable.me

McQueen suggests people run their numbers to work out whether it's a better idea to start with an investment property first.

'One of the biggest mistakes you can make is to take on an unsustainable amount of debt to get into your first home,' she says.

'There may be smarter ways to do it, so make sure you assess your options. And get help if you need it. Property is one of the biggest purchases you will make, so it pays to do it right.'

She says people need to also have a plan. 'Stop kicking "own goals", where your behaviour lets you down, again. Get serious about making progress and become deliberate in building a wealth mindset.'

## David Boyle, past head of investor education at Sorted, now at Mint Asset Management

Boyle says people shouldn't give up. 'Have a budget and stick to it. Knowing where your money is going is the first step to redirecting those savings towards your new home.'

He says people should also make sure they are getting the most out of their KiwiSaver. 'Are you getting your matching employer contributions and the government tax credit, for example? Are you in the right fund for the timeline you have set to buy your first home? If it's going to take ten years to get a deposit together, perhaps a growth fund might be appropriate. If it is less than five years, protect your capital more from market fluctuations and choose a more defensive fund. Get some advice on this.'

He says it's also helpful to find a good mortgage broker. 'They can really help you develop a plan and keep you up to date on housing market movements, while keeping you on track to get that deposit together.'

## Gareth Kiernan, economist and chief forecaster at Infometrics

Kiernan says people should be selective about what they buy and how much they pay.

'Be willing to take more time with your decision-making, because the FOMO has disappeared from the market. And remember that even if prices do dip over the next year or two, you're in it for the long haul, and are likely to be a homeowner for the rest of your life. House price falls might not be an ideal start, but prices will almost certainly recover in future and make any difficulties in the beginning fade in importance.'

## Liz Koh, financial coach

Koh says first-home buyers should remember that their home is not an investment and their first home does not have to be their dream home.

'You can keep your financial stress to a minimum by buying a home that is well within your budget, so that you still have some wriggle room left if interest rates increase or if your income drops. You should plan to still be able to save into an emergency fund so that if you have unexpected expenses you don't need to go into debt.'

## David Whitburn, property developer and investor

Whitburn says first-home buyers should have a medium- and long-term focus, remembering that 'without sacrifice, there is no success'.

He says that when he helps younger people getting ready to buy a house, he is sometimes frustrated by their spending habits.

'If you're going out Friday and Saturday night and blowing the best part of $300, it starts to add up. A sacrifice has to be made. There's not much thought of the long-term consequences – it's too easy to take that text from a friend and go out.'

Many things are out of first-home buyers' control, he says, but one thing in their control is trying to reduce their spending. 'Maybe go out one night instead of two. It was a lot easier for me when I had a $7000 deposit to buy my first home with 5 per cent down in 2002. I have to be mindful of that but the key is to think medium- and long-term, not so much going out and living for the moment but building up those long-term savings.'

## Graeme Fowler, property investor

Fowler says there are a few things that can make the difference between being able to buy and not.

'First of all, rather than visit your own bank, see a good mortgage broker and go over your finances and what you are wanting to achieve,' he says.

'A broker can look at your current situation and determine if there are certain things that you can do now to improve your chances. For example, you may have a car loan of say $5000 and be making weekly payments at high interest on that, and also have savings of $40,000. It may be better to pay off that loan with some of the savings. Also, credit card debt, spending habits, how much you are saving each week, and many other contributing factors may be considered.'

Fowler says a broker can also help you to work out how much deposit you need, and whether you might qualify for a First Home Grant or be able to access your KiwiSaver money.

'If you are ready to buy now and finance is approved subject to finding something suitable, it's a good idea to choose good agents from several different companies in your area and let them know your budget and what you are wanting.

'Often what we end up buying is very different from what we originally thought we wanted. The first property I bought to live in was in the Wellington area. My criterion was a three-bedroom home on the flat with a double garage and at least a 600 square metre section. After looking at hundreds of homes over the next 18 months and finding nothing that I liked, I ended up buying a two-bedroom with a single garage, and cross-leased on a half-section. A big factor for me looking at this place is that it had a fridge and washing machine (neither of which I had) that went with the house! So, often we don't even know what we want ourselves until we find it.

'By looking at a lot of houses for sale and open homes, you will get an idea of prices and what you will likely be able to buy in your price range.'

He says new buyers might have to start with a 25- or 30-year term to meet bank requirements for loan serviceability. But, when it becomes possible, buyers should start to work out ways to reduce the term of the loan by making extra or increased payments. 'The amount of interest you can save by doing this adds up massively.'

## Tony Alexander, independent economist

Alexander urges people not to get hung up on trying to time the market in order to pay the best price for a property, but instead to find a place that suits them, with a vendor who is willing to negotiate.

'People need to think about their first home less as an investment and more as "this is where I make my stand and raise my family". Some people have got a bit lost [thinking] getting on the ladder means getting on the investment ladder as opposed to getting on the rest-of-your-life ladder.'

## Lisa Dudson, financial educator, Acumen

Dudson recommends making a list of what you are looking for, covering the things that are deal-breakers, things that are 'nice to have' and things that you're not really fussed about.

She says this helps to get things clear when you start to look for the right property.

'Do the numbers of various levels of interest rates so you are aware of what it means for your budget if they change. Work with a mortgage adviser to ensure you put some thought into how you structure your mortgage rather than just chasing the lowest interest rate.'

## Jen Baird, chief executive, Real Estate Institute of New Zealand

Baird's advice is simple. 'Line your ducks up, understand as much as you can, and then act with confidence.'

## Katrina Shanks, chief executive, Financial Advice New Zealand

Shanks recommends saving hard through your KiwiSaver and using that as part of your deposit.

'As a first-home buyer you can withdraw all the

KiwiSaver contributions made by you as well as by your employer to use as a deposit, provided you meet three conditions: you have been a KiwiSaver scheme member for at least three years, you will be living in the house for at least six months, and it's your first home.

'The greater your level of contributions you make now the more you will save, so go as hard as you can. Look at areas where you may have wastage every week and see if these can be reduced.'

She says there is no such thing as a 'get-rich-quick scheme' to give you the deposit to buy your first home. 'Don't think cryptocurrencies or share-trading platforms are the answer to maximising your deposit quickly. These are high-risk asset classes.

'You may be eligible for the First Home Loan where you only need a 5 per cent deposit, which means getting into your first home is that much easier. First Home Loans are issued by selected banks and other lenders, and underwritten by Kāinga Ora. This allows the lender to provide loans that would otherwise sit outside their lending standards.

'In addition to KiwiSaver, you may be eligible for a First Home Grant of up to $10,000 per borrower, depending on the cost of the property and income caps being applied.'

She says that if you are struggling to make the figures work, think outside the box. 'Maybe another, longer-term, option is to purchase a house as an investment and rent it out while you rent somewhere else until it increases sufficiently in value when you can sell it for a capital gain to reduce the debt on your next property. This is all in the timing and understanding the tax ramifications, so do your homework first.

'Then there's the friends approach, where you and your mates chip in and contribute to a mortgage instead of paying rent. You may need legal advice to ensure you have all your bases covered for later on if one of you wants to move out.

'The easiest and cheapest way to buy a house is using your parents to guarantee the part of your 20 per cent deposit you don't have.'

## Helen O'Sullivan, chief executive of Crockers Property, formerly at the Real Estate Institute

O'Sullivan says the first thing to do is join KiwiSaver now, if you're not already a member. 'It's a qualifying requirement for some of the assistance programmes and if you're a first-home buyer, you can use some of your KiwiSaver for your deposit. Even if you're only in it for a year, it all helps. If you're buying off the plans, the wait can be long enough to tip you over the two- and three-year anniversaries to increase the assistance you are eligible for.'

She says people should also not be afraid to get into the detail of their finances. 'Do your maths. Set up a spreadsheet, start with your income, track how much you spend on what. Then work out what you can reasonably cut out, allow for costs that you might not be paying in a flatting situation, like maintenance, and be very realistic about what you can afford by way of repayments. That's your budget.'

O'Sullivan urges first-timers not to skimp on research when it comes to finding the right house. 'If you can, find a knowledgeable friend who has purchased before and isn't financially or emotionally involved in your transaction. They can help you navigate the maze of things you need to learn about, keep you company at endless open homes, buy you a drink after another fruitless day searching the web and, most importantly, help you keep to the budget you've set yourself.'

She echoes Koh's message that a first home need not be a forever home. 'Work to what you can reasonably afford at the moment, and expect to transact again, probably more than once, during your property-owning career. So be flexible on suburb and configuration and inflexible on budget. Search realestate.co.nz by price range and go and look at homes in your target city that are in your price range, no matter which suburb they are in. Above all, good luck!'

# ACKNOWLEDGEMENTS

Thanks to all the first-home buyers who shared their stories with me, the economists who answered my endless questions, Michelle Hurley, Kathy Callesen and the Allen & Unwin team, and my husband and my parents for their support.

# ABOUT THE AUTHOR

Susan Edmunds is the business editor at Stuff and was previously its property reporter. She has bought and sold several houses in her life but, as an elderly millennial, she understands what buyers are up against. She is based in Whangarei.